CLASSIFICATION: POETRY

A CIP catalogue record for this book is available from the
British Library.

Printed and bound in Great Britain.
Body text: CG Omega

Paper used in the production of books published by United
Press comes only from sustainable forests.

ISBN 978-0-85781-228-5

First published in Great Britain in 2012 by
United Press Ltd
Admail 3735
London
EC1B 1JB
Tel: 0870 240 6190
Fax: 0870 240 6191
All Rights Reserved
© Copyright contributors 2012

www.unitedpress.co.uk

The Book
Of
Epic Poetry

2012

Foreword

United Press is renowned for producing high quality poetry collections, such as our annual *National Poetry Anthology*, which contain poems of an easily digestible length.

However, there are those themes that are simply too large to explore in 160 words, and some poets need the freedom to fully express their creativity. Epic and long poems give them the opportunity to do this without constraint.

This anthology, *The Book of Epic Poetry*, is the result of talent on a grand scale; each writer within these pages has quite literally gone to great lengths to express their vision in words, and with impressive results. So it is with great pleasure that we present this compilation, and we hope that you find as much enjoyment in the art form as we have.

Joanna Cummings, Editor

Contents

The poets who have contributed to this volume are listed below, along with the relevant page upon which their work can be found.

11	Michelle Layton	87	Maurice Sangan
15	Steven Bown	88	Pamela Foster
17	Betty Brooksby	89	Joan Facey
20	Heather Buswell	90	David Grayling
22	Jack Rossiter	91	Peter W Clayton
25	Mark Cory	92	Ruth Miller
28	Nell Thompson	93	Philip Chadwick
34	Lee Hughes	94	Janet Rogers
37	Iris D Turner	95	Anthony P Thomas
39	Malcolm Benjamin	96	Patrick O'Shaughnessy
43	Peter Morriss	97	Mark Cory
47	Ronnie Kilgore	99	Steven Bown
53	Dorothy Gerrard	100	Rosemarie Lynn Foulkes
56	Karen Walker	101	Terry Bednall
58	Joan Lake	102	Edna Glew
62	Leslie Scrase	103	George Sutton
65	Richard Land	105	Betsy Tench
68	Sandra Goddard	106	John Parry
69	Lorraine Williams	107	Edith Anderson
72	Di Bagshawe	108	Verna Broadhurst
73	Dorothy Gerrard	109	Margaret Hunter
74	Pauline Rust	110	Kathy Wilson
75	Leslie Scrase	111	Janette Patterson
77	Violetta Jean Ferguson	112	Tony Sainsbury
78	Beryl Leece	113	Carol Smithard
79	June Squires	114	Patricia Barnicott
80	Richard Land	116	Jack Barnetson
81	Ann McNair	117	Grace Ball
82	Pamela Davies	118	Shirley Wescombe
83	Lance Barnwell	119	Peggy Rolland
84	Elizabeth Harding	120	John Carr
86	Kevin Andrews	121	Bruce Martin

122 Betty Fenton
123 Charles Adams
124 Joan Kernick
124 Yvonne Stanley
126 Christopher Bragg
127 Margaret Burtenshaw-Haines
128 Hazel Oliver
129 Patricia Clark
130 Alicja Smith
131 Patricia Tausz
132 Eileen Mills
134 Annette Taylor
135 Elizabeth Stockhill
137 Terence Crowley
138 David A Smith
139 Avril Lansdell
140 Margaret Jorgensson
141 Catherine Moran
142 David K Maxwell
144 Georgia Machin
144 Hugh G Griffiths
145 Peter Young
146 Suzette Lindsay

GIRLS' NIGHT OUT

We signal the barman - we've decided
We won't have any more
As it is I'm having trouble negotiating
As the pink elephant escorts us to the door

Our raucous karaoke rendition
Of Abba's *Dancing Queen*
Got us noticed earlier
And it's now time to leave the scene

I'm the captain on a cruise ship
My stomach's full of eels
My four-inch stiletto has absconded
From my pair of new high heels

They're dangling coyly from my finger
As we try to hail a cab
The *trip and rip* that wrecked my tights
Is going to leave a scab

I make a mental note
To write a snotty letter
To whoever laid the pavement
They could have done it better

I wonder if the same person
Who made sure the road was skew.
Will be kind enough to replace
The heel on my left shoe

While pondering this prospect
There is a loud uproar
Sophie's bag has just exploded
Spilling its contents on the floor

All the girls are giggling
And tottering precariously about

As the taxi pulls up next to us
Sophie gives an outraged shout

You've killed my compact.
That's a hit and run!
Sophie's in full attack mode
And her temper's set on stun

At first the jaded driver
Doesn't bat an eye
He's yet to learn that Sophie's
Not one to let things lie

After five long minutes
Of her expletive-filled rebuff
The taxi driver is on his hands and knees
Picking up all her stuff

With decorum out the window
We all bundle into the car
Flashing knickers and attracting
A large audience from the bar

Amy's busy exchanging numbers
With a hottie she just snogged
But we know they'll never hook up
If the digits have been jogged!

As we pull off from the kerb
We catch sight of Amy's face
She's looking kind of clownish
With her lipstick out of place

I glance sideways at Hannah
As we set off into the night
Her pallor's slightly greenish
And a bucket's not in sight

I tap the driver on his arm

And ask him please to hurry
But Amy's had a bright idea
To stop and get a curry

My tummy lurches at the thought
It's already playing tricks
The Jägerbombs and Shooters
Were not a clever mix

It takes some persuading
To change Amy's sozzled mind
But finally the curry's vetoed
Sometimes it's crueller to be kind

We're all on a come-down now
The taxi's hot and steaming
I can't wait to get home to my bed
Where I can do some dreaming

Still marvelling at our transport
It's like a four-wheeled sauna
We screech to the first sudden stop
Narrowly escaping head trauma

First stop is Hannah's stop
We all have to lend assistance
To extricate our nauseous friend
Who's far from going the distance

It's the first of many teetering walks
From taxi to front door
With stifled giggles, lots of cursing
And one gin-soaked loud guffaw

We all get dropped off one by one
Amid drunken hugs and kisses
I'm sure our driver's quite relieved
To get rid of all us misses

I'm the last to be delivered
And by default pay the fare
The cabbie must by now, be tipsy
From breathing alcohol-fumed air

In the dark I think he winks at me
He looks that type of bloke,
But I'm feeling far from amorous
I'm drunk and now I'm broke.

As I tumble hastily from the cab
My DIY headache starts to hammer
But to the driver, in the review mirror
I am *the epitome of glamour*

I stagger up to my front door
And fumble for my key
I wish the door would just stop moving
And cooperate with me

I drop everything in the hallway
Throw my keys into the dish
And in my state, by mistake
Feed cornflakes to the fish

I realise far too late
That I've mixed up Nemo's dinner
He'll either go belly-up by the morning
Or drop one dress size and be slimmer

Guiltily I bowl examine
The little orange guy
He seems to be in no distress
And hope he doesn't die

I say *goodnight* and kill the lights
Undressing as I cross the floor
My ears are ringing, my mouth is dry
And my blistered feet are sore

I take a shower and brush my teeth
And fall into my bed
But before I close my eyes
Just one thought goes through my head

Though we have good fun, the girls and I
On our girls' night out
The raging hangover that visits me
Is one I'd rather be without

So I resign myself to a day ahead
Of feeling out of shape
And swallow paracetamol
Like Bacchus eating grapes

Michelle Layton, Wellington, Herefordshire

THE WAY NOT TAKEN

Back door opens, come on wench, chop chop
Weer's mi tea? In t'coral sea?
Yer spend t'dee wi t' 'ead in geography books,
Weer's mi slop? Still darn't shop?
I order thee by royal decree
To feed me, king of castle, the breadwinner,
Me, me, me!

Ay, that's nor we t'address e lady!
'M not yer slave, stuff you, am off to a rave
Bi back by midnight, maybe, don't wait up
T'meal's burnt, won't save
Gooin' f' sum musical 'n' spirital solace,
Meditation I crave.

Ay! Wot time du yer call this, miss?
Cumin' in all hours, dirty stop aart
Bet y've bin accostin' por unsuspectin' blokes,
In wedded bliss.

Cheap, park bench dwellin' hussy, common taart!

Makeshift feminist, knees 'im in t'crunch, *Ow!*
Quells 'is marine marriage tackle 'n' sexual prowess
Watch it or there'll bi regicide 'n' all t'other reggies besides.

Goes to prove, faint 'eart never won fair lady, 'owever shady.
Not the way to go, Joe!

By chance, out of the eerie mist
Of mice and men created,
The antagonistic works of nature persist,
Challenged of the dark distant past, permeated:
But where to go?
Long awaited trials and tribulations,
Troubles and natural catastrophes, befell nations,
Spiritual callings to the masses,
Political, religious crises seemingly reached impasses:
Cravings for large, medium, even minute mercies,
Would their prayers be answered?
Hopefully bring a halt to global controversies,
Would military strikes, by super power, interventions,
Bring a surgical solution, obliterate terminal ablation?
Surely not.

Attacks on Iran
Will only serve to sever main arteries,
A Middle-East bloodbath,
The final suturing up, not performed with much artistry.
Prestige, with influence of government autonomies
Showed human frailties, as tired in vain to interact,
Clumsy, inept attempts to prop up economies
Used dumbed down policies of antimatter, of dubious fact
All this in the name of democracies, by fascist dictators
Not just of the former Warsaw Pact,
The rise of the Orwellian little people, to extract.

So Katrina had struck, with all her hellbent fury,
Left a deluge, huge lake not fit for a duck,

The jukeboxes of New Orleans held to judgment by
The hurricane's destructive jury,
While Bush slept peacefully in his ranch,
His mate God reaped havoc, like a K2 avalanche.
Christian men, wearing cassocks,
Their loyalties and beliefs
Stubborn, hard as rocks, evangelists that tend to their flocks
Tsunamis stir, under the earth, quakes and aftershocks,
All seemed settled for a while,
Was this the calm before the storm?
Like a Greek tragedy, to the world stage,
Actors gathered to perform, then suddenly, a lightning bolt,
The Holy Spirit, but what was this?

Ours was not to reason why, his miracles and wonders,
Oh dear, for our blunders. Sorry Oh Lord!

Steven Bown, Chesterfield, Derbyshire

THE TURNING YEAR

Spring
Gone is winter with its cold winds,
With its bitter chills and snow storms;
Banished are the blasts of winter,
Grey, cold winter, foggy winter.
Winter sleeps, whilst earth awakens.

In the woodland, in the springtime,
In the green and moisty woodland,
There the things of nature waken,
Waken to the warming sun rays.
There the bracken spirals upwards,
Curls her ribboned fronds about her.
Snowdrop, shy, in green seclusion,
Modest snowdrop, wears her bonnet;
White and green, she greets the new year;
Heralds in the changing seasons,
Bids farewell to winter's wildness,

Hails the coming of the springtime.
And the bluebell spreads her carpet,
Spreads her woodland's magic cover
'Neath the budding trees and hedgerows
Where new life is fast a-stirring.

In the woodland, tiny creatures,
Birds and bees and furry creatures,
Waken to the new year's trumpet;
Start to call, to sing, to chatter,
Start to waken to the sunshine.

Valley, field and mountain pasture,
Coloured new in springtime palette;
Green and gold and blue and yellow,
Please the eye with nature's beauty.

Summer
Now the sun begins to cheer us.
Gentle zephyrs, freshening breezes,
Carry forth the scents of rebirth.
Summer's azure skies foretelling
Days of leisure, warm and pleasant;
Days of sunshine, joy and laughter.
Shadows dapple fields and hedgerows.

Gently flow the streams and rivers;
Rivers where the salmon leap and
Water boatmen skim the surface.
And from the banks, the mossy banks,
Where the reeds and willows flourish,
Water creatures, rat and beaver,
See all nature sliding by them.
Carried on the rippling waters,
Through the woodlands, by the meadows,
Sleepy hamlets, busy cities,
Flotsam from the great high mountains
Swirling onwards on its journey;
There to meet the big sea waters,

There to join the big salt waters,
On the currents of the ocean,
Forth into the great unknown.

Autumn
Sadly, as the days grow cooler,
Shadows lengthen, days grow shorter;
Gone the beauteous fragrant blossoms,
Gone the scents of summer past.

In the woodlands, in the forests,
Autumn brings the smell of wood smoke,
Chop of blade and squeak of cartwheel,
As the coppice and the hedgerow
Bow before the woodman's axe.
Trees adorned with jewelled crowns,
Orchards bowed beneath their burden;
Nuts and fruit, abundant harvest,
Golden fields of corn and barley,
Signal autumn's dying glory.

Winter
In the woodland, in the winter,
In the dark and dismal winter,
Trees laid bare to winter's fury
Stretch their branches to the heavens.

Where the sap is running thinly
Leaves now fallen, brown and crinkled,
Tumbled to the cooling earth;
Skeletons of leaves long withered
Fallen from their mother bough,
Gone their glory, gone their splendour,
Protecting earth beneath them now.

Stone cold winter, cruel winter
Steals upon us, bleak and hoary;
Spreads its tentacles about us
Gripping all in dance macabre.

19

Short the days and long the dark nights.
Sharp and searching blow the cold winds.

Gone the sun beyond the hilltops,
Gone to rest beyond the mountains.
And the moon in silvery splendour
Creeps above the far horizon,
Whilst the stars, in myriad beauty,
Look to earth and shed their light.
Where the ice and snow have fallen
Winter reigns in a sea of white.

And so throughout the long cold season
Nature sleeps, in waiting lies;
Waiting for the great awakening -
Warmer days and bluer skies.

Da Capo.

Betty Brooksby, Halifax, West Yorkshire

IN LIMBO

Once, in the beginning, there was me,
Young, wild and free,
And able to feel
So much, for a man I thought was real.
That was not you.
All that was true
Was one of the faces of the psyche.

And now, I realise that I never knew
All the real you,
Only loved so much
The aspect I believed to be such,
When that phase died,
How long I tried
To resurrect the man who never was.

I sought him in times future and past,
In worlds so vast,
So twisted and deep
I could not understand, could not keep
Even myself,
Even the wealth
Of my personality, intact.

Trying, always to find, in me,
Some sort of key.
Myself a stranger
To me, loving an unknown stranger.
I was too lost
To count the cost
Of caring for a soul in limbo.

I, a projectile shot into space,
Cannot find grace
Enough to endure
The burning of ice, to make me pure,
Life is too fleet,
I can't compete
With things, and walls of indifference.

I can't break through to find the real you,
Or find the you
Whom I have once known,
Nor find I, who was me, alone.
I don't know how,
Except that now
I read my sorrows in reflection,

See my loneliness in another.
April lover,
So gentle and kind,
I know you, too, are trying to find
The you, you knew,
I know you too
Must be another soul in limbo.

I, who am now so young, yet so old,
Need not be told
I have not met you,
But love a phase you are going through.
Some day, you'll find
Your own true mind,
And then you may no longer need me.

I know the man you really are,
Maybe so far
Removed from me,
That there could be no affinity,
Shall I again
Seek love in vain?

My God! Is nobody ever real?

Heather Buswell, Newton Abbot, Devon

FIVE HUNDRED STEPS

There stood a foul and filthy fort; all gentleness it smote;
An Age of Dark, and bitter tears, had channelled out the moat.
Of all bent centuries it scourged, the thirteenth was most dire,
For therein dwelt Lord Effingham, and Blindingham, his squire.
Five hundred steps above the land, the lord leered to the left;
No one now lived on that land that had not been Lord-Effed:
Full rude he had undone them, seized their very chattels,
But like the cat with the conked-out mouse, still bristled for more
battles.
So Blindingham must blight more souls, ravage them to plaguery;
Go yourself, you big rich stinker, he muttered with some bravery.
The lord picked up the poker: *You'll dance if you refuse!*
I see defiance in your eye - and poo upon your shoes.
So Blindingham adventured forth across the silent wides,
To seek out aught that may be brought to grief and woe betides.
Winter sun slouched on the hedge he rode his old nag by,
Until the tower had dwindled to a misprint on the sky.
Long the trail, and sly the byways, sloggardly the land;

The ageing day set down to doze, and gold had left the sand.
But morning brought entrancement as he sat and sucked his thumb:
A lady sweet as summer showers, and kind to creatures dumb.
Lest the snake should shed its skin, she fastened it with pegs;
On parrots from the pirate ships she fitted wooden legs;
She flipped the squirrel from the tree, tended its sore paw;
Blindingham skunked back to tell his master what he saw.
Alas it was her kindness that proved the maid's undoing:
For as she fed the animals at next noontide there flew in
A big besmotted buzzard, of all gracefulness bereft,
With tattywagging hinderparts, and leering to the left.
It skulked and smarmed for breadcrumbs, while at the Lady's back
Approached the baleful Blindingham to snare her in a sack.
The Lady's supple movements, as she stooped and stood to feed,
Confused the ever-waiting squire, who in his ill-judged speed
Rushed in to take her prisoner, but snared instead his lord:
A sack on that malignant pate, O Saints! A just reward!
And yet she saw it not so: with pity for the weak
She rescued the unhappy bird, who, pestilent with pique,
Rained blows upon his servant's head until this latter cried,
Arroint thee, tyrant, lest we lose our conquest and our prize!
The master froze; remembered now the next part of the ruse,
And, leering to the left, approached the Lady, now bemused,
Plucked from his cloak a poppy, a bent and gory thing,
One breath of whose obnoxious tip the swooning soul doth fling To
wakelessness. So dark fell on the Flower,
And she was taken prisoner to Effingham's dread tower.
The Lady had a Champion, a Blade of Shining Steel,
Who waited by her window at evening churchbells' peal,
Then morning's and midday's. At last he called his ward;
My Lady's gone! Fetch me my horse! - A poor substitute, my lord?
Long the trail and sly the byways, day nor night gave rest;
Dark for sleep as darkest woods they quaked not on their quest.
Thin old moon hunched up and shivered over shadows on the road;
They came to where she had to be: Lord Effingham's abode.
For their ingress they deemed it best a strategem employ
Known to warriors ancient as the Wooden Horse of Troy.
With fitful speed they built one to stand beneath the walls:
It bequeathed the Lady Effingham a stand to hang her smalls.

Undaunted by this setback, the brave ward donned a gown
She'd laid there; so bedraggled, he kept his head well down.
Sure enough, the rain fell; her ladyship harked back
And took him with her raiments into that fortress black.
Outside his master lay concealed while danger was about:
Five hundred steps above him Lord Effingham looked out, Leering
long unto the left 'til rain obscured his sight:
Himthinks he has ahead of him a really dirty night.
Anon the Maid from sleep's dark shade was due to make a show;
He hastened in; the ward hallooed his master from below,
Threw him a stalwart tether, which, once securely bound,
He pulled with all his manhood; an unknown strength he found To
heave his master upwards, when, the task but all achieved,
He heard a footstep near him, and, unteachable, relieved
The rope to which his master clung, to send him lightning-quick
Plunging endlong to the moat. Thinks he, *Oh, fiddlesticks.*
But onward came those footsteps; the ward looked round in dread
And hid in an adjoining room, in truth, within the bed,
Deeming to be safe inside this refuge he'd discovered,
And did not see our Heroine, from sleep still unrecovered.
Full blown from his excursions, he took his place beside her:
He wot not what lot he'd got, and she did not know neither.
The door leered open with an evil cackle: we envisage ...
Effingham! Arrived to taste the sweet fruits of his pillage.
He seized the young ward's person: *These oxsters feel not right!*
But hush! He heard his wife's approach, and from this parlous plight
Thought underneath the coverlets a meet means of concealment;
Alas for him, his wife espied a double-dire revealment:
Two harlots in his bed, begad! The rake must surely die!
She pummelled his patellas - but - what's this hue and cry?
A doleful discord floods the fort, that wails of faithlessness.
Lady Eff herself took flight, and - did you guess?
Hid in bed beside her lord. Now all await the tread
Approaching up five hundred steps, 'til just above the bed
A figure stood. The bedmates screamed; our Heroine awoke:
Behold, her noble Champion! Yet he could only choke -
She could not undishonoured be with bedfellows ensconced.
I'll slit you tongues of snakes! Lie still! he thundercracks at once.
But ere the bedfolk could respond there came that wail outside, So

godless and of ill intent, our Hero made to hide
In bed. *No!* cried Effingham. *It must have been my man.*
There's five of us inside the room. The sixth is Blindingham.
Pray pardon, sire, but 'twasn't I, a voice below them said,
And Blindingham, a cur to kick, skunked out below the bed.
He'd been hoping to enjoy the maid before his lord had come:
Silly sorry, sire, quoth he, and sucked his silly thumb.
But whence that hideous howling then? whimpered Lady Effingham.
Our Hero spake: *On thirteenth days, in months that have an F in them,*
The devil calls to claim one soul, and hence he's here tonight.
Annoyful misborns that you are, I urge you to take flight.
I met him not upon the stair; he scales the walls outside;
In silence let us scatter. God speed you where you hide.
They nipped behind the arras, they entered grots and graves,
The cavities and recesses, false panels, crypts and caves;
Behind the smelly deerskin, the coffer you still smell it on;
Blindingham nipped in a niche, and got kicked out by a skeleton.
Lord Effingham took to the stairs to flee that fearful fort,
One hundred and fifteen, he counts, too numb for any thought,
Four hundred and, er thirty two... his mind must not play tricks..
Six hundred and sixty-five and a half ... six hundred and sixty ... six

Jack Rossiter, Waltham Cross, Hertfordshire

FOURTEEN HOURS

Brekpups, brekpups, brekpups: breakfast's ready,
My mother's voice is singing up the stairs.
Perched on my bed, I jerk my feet into my shoes.
A good firm bed with solid walls around.
A polished boarded floor, with green and yellow rug.
The yellow spines of all my Rupert books,
On the top shelf; a row of twenty-one.
Below, Grimm's Fairy Tales: Hans Anderson.

Across in France they're fuelling up another flying-bomb.
Hitler's revenge weapon: does he know where Banstead is?
This one's lined up towards Nork Shops: our house is just next door.

Jumping up, I race into the bathroom;
Splash some cold water up across my face,
And clatter down into the frying smell of bacon.
I eat alone at breakfast, hurrying down my food.
Father's still coming back from London night work;
My sister still asleep, but I have weekend school.

Goodbye, a quick kiss from my mother and I'm on my way.
Must not be late for school; I pedal fast.
It is a bright and sunny July morning.

In France the flying-bomb sits waiting for the off.

Breathless, but I'm well in time for morning prayers,
And while we sing the hymn to start the day,
The waiting Doodlebug is activated.

The ram-jet engine rips apart the silence of the fields.
The dark shape of the bomb lifts to the silvery, sunny air,
Its tail jet burning white against the morning light.

Prayers are over, our row leads out to start our lesson.
We settle to the scratching sounds of pen on paper.
But now the distant sirens, then our own one wails.
Stand up, hitch gas mask over shoulder: walk, don't run.

Clattering down the wooden stairs, we file into the shelter.
It's quiet and dark and shadows dance;
Flickering candles burning high along the passages.
Quiet murmured talk, while every ear is listening.

I rest my back against the cool and solid cement wall.
Suddenly the concrete slams against my shoulders,
And then a double shock wave punches in across my stomach.
Now, unexplained, a cold and overwhelming feeling;
I'm sure my house is hit, I say out loud.
Peter Webb beside me looks into my eyes.
Your house? He sees I am distressed.
I'm sure that was my house, I say again.

All clear is sounding; we lead up to the light.
Headmaster grabs my arm and pulls me from the line.
Your family is alright: your father's here. Your house was hit.

Into the head's study; my father standing there.
No shoes, his city suit pockmarked with little tears.
Everyone's alright, he says: *The house is gone.*
No house: a pile of wreckage capped by slowly rising dust;
And we are left with just the clothes we're wearing.

Peter Nevard's mother takes us in.
She gives us lunch and finds a pair of shoes to fit my father.
Then down to Banstead Station past the sunlit tower of dust,
Still rising from the wreckage of our house.
My little tree, I'd watched grow daily, blown away.
Not yet sunk in how lucky both my parents and my sister.
The growling of the flying-bomb had ceased abruptly.
My mother, cooking Father's breakfast, had not heard.
One's cut out quite close, my Father shouts.
Walk quickly to the front room shelter.
There, in the Morrison, our dog is crouching.
Suddenly a sense of acute danger and they run.
The very second that they throw themselves inside,
Beneath the strong protecting sheet of steel, the house collapses.
How did Larry the red setter know?

Part of one wall remains, the dog leads out.
Crawling, they follow, through the dust.
People outside, amazed to see them scrambling out.
It seems impossible to come unscathed from out the flattened house.
And now we're on our way to Devonshire.
My Father's rung my uncle and we're going back;
Back to the house at Beauchamp, our haven from the earlier raids.

Exeter St David's Station and Uncle Tommy's there to welcome us.
It's dark and soon we're on the road to Tiverton.
Wedged safely in the back seat, only half awake;
The steady engine's drone and above us sliding by,
Great tree branches, lit silver by a brilliant moon.

Past ten o'clock we pull into the yard.
At Beauchamp everyone is still awake.
My seven cousins all agog to see and hear.
First a quick meal and off we are to bed.
No luggage to unpack, no brush to brush our teeth,
It's all so quiet and peaceful after Banstead's hostile skies.
Robin and I both talk a bit: I start to drift to sleep;
It's all running through my mind: Banstead's a world away.
Only fourteen hours ago, I was leaving home for school.

Mark Cory, Banstead, Surrey

A MODERN DAY MIRACLE

On the west coast of South America
Is a narrow strip of land
2700 miles long - called Chile,
Includes a patch of desert sand.

It is called the Atacama Desert,
And far below the ground,
In the bowels of the earth
The San Jose mine is found,

Thirty three miners went down,
To work as usual that day,
But 700,000 tons of rock fell in,
Which meant they were there to stay.
It hit them like a thunderbolt,
The shock was so severe,
The human mind found it hard to grasp
Their hearts were filled with fear.

The news soon reached their homes,
Parents, wives and children all,
Distressed, saddened, crying.
Loved ones beyond their call.

They knew hopes of rescue were bleak,

Trapped in the San Jose mine,
Half a mile from earth's surface,
Not a ray of hope could they find.

No doubt, immediate action;
Plans were made without delay,
With powerful drilling machinery,
They worked hard, night and day.

Loved ones visited the surface,
Anguish rose with each passing day,
The worries of starvation,
Filled them with dismay.

One major problem was food,
How could they survive?
Three days supply of tuna soup,
For seventeen days kept them alive!

The miners listened and listened,
Faint sounds from the drill they could hear,
They were filled with delight and euphoria,
To see a small bore hole appear.

The long silence was broken
News to relatives was quickly relayed,
Telling the good news gladly,
Men all alive, it said.

Words can't explain the excitement,
At last a ray of hope,
For relations and friends, it comfort meant,
And helped them all to cope.

This was very welcome news,
With mixed feelings was received,
Rescue still seemed far away,
But somehow they felt relieved.

Never were men more thankful
To receive at last some food,
Through this five and a half inch bore hole of mercy
Nourishment - it tasted so good.

This communication was vital,
In constant use each day,
Bringing much needed necessities,
From half a mile away.

At the mine head, scores of reporters
Circulated news to read and see,
To a world that was watching and waiting,
That miners would soon be set free.

Workmen continued boring,
Plans in hand, A, B and C.
When A had been exhausted,
They turned then to Plan B.

After heavy pressure drilling,
The drill breaks in the hole
Causing unwanted breakdown,
And delay to reach the goal.

The work has been fraught with problems,
All along the way.
Plan C was brought into use,
And that sure saved the day.
Workforce was so coordinated,
Specific plans were all agreed,
Expertise in action,
For the venture to succeed.

Meanwhile the boring continued,
And another group worked too,
Building a suitable capsule,
As a means of release for the crew.

Jose Henrique - one of the miners,
Was a part time evangelist too,
Who ministered to their spiritual need;
The caring thing to do.

Each man had a miniature Bible,
Jose held studies twice each day,
To bring consolation and comfort,
And hope as each one would pray.

There was a loud drilling noise - vibration,
Suddenly strong fumes filled the air,
At last, the massive drill broke through,
So welcome to men in despair.

Words cannot describe the scene,
All filled with happiness and delight.
They danced, and hugged each other,
It was such a moving sight.

After sixty-eight long weary days,
The future now seemed bright,
The thoughts of loved ones and home,
And to see once more daylight.

The phoenix capsule, thirteen feet tall,
Small wheels around in place,
A strong wire rope was then attached,
To bring men from the base.

In colours of the Chilean flag,
It was painted red, white and blue,
Twenty one and a half inches it measured across,
With a video camera to view.

Then there was assistance
Of the paramedics, who
Were lowered down the mine shaft,
To see what they could do.

Manuel Gonzalez - a mine inspector
Went down to lend his aid,
And make a brief inspection,
As the final plans were made.

The preparation was so meticulous,
It is evident at a glance,
Every imaginable precaution was taken,
So nothing was left to chance.

Each man was given light clothing,
Safety harness and oxygen in case,
Breathing would be difficult,
In such a confined space.

A video camera to check panic attacks,
A microphone and earpiece to tell,
With a monitor to check heart, pulse and breathing,
To indicate if all was well.

Claustrophobia - I wonder?
In a rock-hole twenty one inches wide,
Escape was the only answer,
So on this, they did decide.

On the thirteenth of October at midnight,
The big rescue venture began,
While the world was watching and waiting,
To see the release of each man.

Florencio Avalos was first,
Tense, nervous and shy,
Thrilled, at last he landed
Looked pale, with a tear in his eye.

Sebastain Pinera - the Chilean President
Was there to welcome everyone,
An expression of his concern for them,
And see how well they'd done.

One miner came from Bolivia,
A faithful worker and true,
So the Bolivian president came,
And was there to welcome him too.

The miners emerged in identical t-shirts,
Printed on the front, the message was clear,
Thank You Lord, and the Chilean flag,
Thanks expressed for arrival here.

On the back was a quote from Psalm 95,
The depths of the earth in God's hand,
The mountain peaks belong to Him
His creation is so grand.

What scenes of jubilation,
As they sang and clapped and cheered,
The sound echoed from the mountains,
'Til the last man had appeared.

When all the miners congregated,
They flew ten minutes to land
At Capioca Hospital,
To have health checks as planned.

These health checks were recorded,
And complaints were very few,
The doctors, they were all amazed,
Seeing what these men came through.

Discharged, each man went to his home,
What joy and welcome there,
And so much love and happiness,
In answer to their prayer.

Back to the gold and copper mine,
No one will ever go,
The government have closed it down,
They simply have said, *No*.

Finally, we acknowledge,
The skillfulness of man,
And thank the God of Miracles,
For His part in the plan.

Nell Thompson, County Antrim, Northern Ireland

ONE DREAMY DAY

We did wile away one hot summer day.
In a boat, on a river, through fields of hay.
A nice glass of wine 'neath the golden sunshine.
Strawberries and cream for my love and I.
She wore a straw hat, a white dress that flowed,
And the biggest of smiles for me to behold.
She had a parasol of brilliant white.
Cooled, in shade, from the bright sunlight.
I looked in her eyes, I was mesmerised
As I placed my hands on her inner thighs.
She sat there on the cushioned chair.
Suggestion beckoned in the air.
Containing desires was something anew.
As we fantasised of things we might do.
The sun shone down on her silky dress.
A light breeze did make her nipples erect.
Her blonde hair moved with majestic sway.
A beautiful sight, akin to the hay.
She was breathing shallow as I neared her face.
Her pupils grew large. My pulse, it raced.
I closed my eyes as I kissed her lips.
My hands fell upon her slender hips.
I did not want to stop, I could not retract,
As I slid my arms around her back.
My tongue touched hers, a taste so sweet.
Our boundaries were making a hasty retreat.
My hand touched her breast; she drew a sharp breath.
I was dizzy with lust under her arrest.
Her hand found my cheek with a gentle stroke.
From deep inside her pleasure spoke.

Her slightest moan escaped from within.
I sighed with joy. She gave me a grin.
I re-took my seat and began to row.
Half carried along by the river's flow.
I breathed in the air, it was fresh and clear.
We meandered along, the moments were dear.
And a butterfly rested upon the boat's stern.
To take stock of the day which, no doubt, it had earned.
A honey bee, donned in pollen, passed by.
Its sound filled my ears; its flight caught my eye.
Away it went on a mazy course.
Back to his queen, for she's his life source.
Throned right there in front of me.
I looked upon my very own queen.
I am a soldier to all her needs.
Much like my friend the honey bee.
The landscape had changed, I barely knew.
Lost in the moment, we lovers two.
Fields turned green, the aromas were lush.
The sight could have fallen from an artist's brush.
We moored by a jetty on the river's edge.
I held her hand and up she stepped.
She walked on at a leisurely pace.
Her movement floated with such refined grace.
I grabbed our things and set off behind.
She peered over her shoulder with a look so kind.
As I caught her up, she put her hand in mine
A quick kiss to celebrate this wonderful time.
She led me on to long reeds of grass.
We lay down a blanket, away from the path.
She sat at first and I glanced down.
I must have looked lost, as she gave me a frown.
Her hand held aloft, she offered it to me.
I kissed its back, the fragrance was sweet.
So I knelt beside her, her straw hat fell.
I put my lips on her and it felt well.
I unzipped her dress, oh, that silken gown
My hands on her shoulders, I laid her down.
She slipped it off with the greatest of ease.

I unbuttoned my shirt as she pulled at the sleeves.
She removed my pants and we lay bare.
I embraced the moment without a care.
The long grass swayed from the breeze above.
My blood rushed, I was about to make love.
Her body arched as she stuck out her chest.
I pushed my knee between her legs.
They opened up like a sun-touched flower.
She lay in wait for me to devour.
I shifted my body in a tender move.
As I touched her between, it was silky smooth.
I entered her body, we both inhaled.
Any hidden emotion was being unveiled.
I glided, at first, with a gentle flow.
Kissing her breast as I moved to and fro.
My excitement grew, my muscles were tense.
The rush of the feeling was so immense.
Her face was a picture, she tightened her grip.
A slight moan of pleasure as she bit her lip.
I moved more rapid, we gathered momentum.
It was close to explosive, I was arriving in heaven.
She kept saying, *Yes*, this drove me on.
Her juices were flowing, I felt so strong.
The moment was here, my heart pounded fast.
I was shook to my heels, I could no longer last.
With my hands on the floor I arched my back.
We screamed for each other as we both climaxed.
We lay for a while in each other's hold.
Our bodies still shaking from the moments of gold.
Her skin was so smooth, her lips so tender.
I was kissing her gently. Such a thing to remember.
We rolled around all naked and free.
She is the dearest thing to me.
I told her I loved her with definite feeling.
She said the same and my soul was reeling.
We threw on some clothes and put our things away.
Ambled slowly with the summer day.
The shadows were long and the heat was subsiding.
A group of kids flew past us riding.

Shouting and laughing and wet from a swim.
Music to our ears. It was a beautiful thing.
The red sun was fat and hung low in the skies.
This hazy day shimmered and blurred my eyes.
An arm round each other, in such a nice place.
We walked down a winding single track lane.
A car came along and the driver waved.
We gave her a smile and she was on her way.
A dragonfly whizzed in frantic flight.
To find its resting place for the night.
The sun was now falling, halved by horizon.
Our skin was cooling. Goosebumps arising.
We got to our car. She opened the door.
When we got in, we kissed once more.
So off we set on the long drive home.
Red skin bodies from our naked roll.
We'd had a wonderful time all day long.
And now on the radio played a beautiful song.
That spoke about lovers having the best of times.
It reflected the day and we sang out its rhymes.
With all my heart I can honestly say.
She made this one dreamy day.

Lee Hughes, Ellesmere Port, Cheshire

ALL ABOARD FOR A KENTISH DELIGHT!

I'm not sure what I was looking for when I climbed aboard.
Nor that the beauty of Kent would be my reward.
A coach trip in spring can be a disaster or pure delight
Maybe a reward for a good deed or a complete opposite.

Make of it what you will as you feel inclined.
Beauty soon is passed or could be a state of mind.
All I know is what I saw, it was so beautiful to me.
So join me if you will on a trip through my fair county.

It's all aboard past outposts of houses with neat gardens matched.
Speed on to where roads join fields and houses thatched.

Onward to blackthorn hedges in bloom, giving way to gorse.
Past a field with ponies and rabbits huddled to avoid a horse.

Rabbits decided to hip and hop, one cleaned an ear!
Horse wasn't interested and the ponies came not near.
On and on sped the coach past fields where corn was green.
Past a field of oilseed rape, the best crop I'd seen.

Along the verges we now pass, dandelions and daisies stand fast.
Bordering fields of varying shades of green with bird life flying
past
A pheasant walking past in gaudy colouring outshone the
surrounding green.
He was the most exotic character we had yet to encounter or seen.

The fields changed to woods as onward we sped, colours muted
now.
Suddenly emerged bluebells nodding their heads in a seeming
bow.
An ocean of blue flowers looking like colouring of a tropical sea.
The rooks on high, cawing loud, sounding like a malevolent glee.

The trees thinned, timber-framed houses came into view.
With well kept gardens and lilacs of varying hues.
Such a lot for an odd job gardener to manage and control.
Including getting rid of the magpie on top of a pole.

We travel past a village church standing proud and tall.
God's acre filled with memorial stones, moss and lichen covers
all.
It was such peaceful spot for a countryman to lie.
The dead slept well in the hallowed ground we passed by.

Onward yet again past a well rounded Kentish Oast
Alas Kentish hops no longer allowed to toast.
It's now a much admired dwelling place of high renown.
Set in a piece of post-neolithic Kentish Down.

At the end of the lane we turn to the right

A notice board advertising an opera is in sight.
The sheep in its field are not classically inclined.
Their idea of singing is limited to *Baa* - but never mind.

As we return from our objective A Stately Home.
We follow a different route a shorter way to roam.
It's past a handmade fence guarding a verdant field ...
Suddenly the landscape undulates, then part is concealed.

A stream runs to the left of the field with Lilliputian banks
Which thrust and turn and a heron gulps and gives thanks ...
The stream flowed on like us, with a more gentle turn of speed.
Unlike us it had no need to observe or follow as we lead.

Flashing by, we gather speed and will soon be gone.
The stagnant pool at the edge of the trees will linger on and on.
Gathering speed now to head for the distant motorway.
A fitting ending to a perfectly happy Kentish day.

Iris D Turner, Herne Bay, Kent

IT CAME FROM BENEATH

The slumbering city awoke to an unforgettable, unforgiving dawn,
with a natural disaster expressing wrath and horror borne.
Hell had no fury like the earthquake scorned,
underground and overground the merciless beast adorned.
An ominous rumbling roar from the depths of the earth,
had quivered a few miles out, under the sea.
After a seismic foreshock had preceded in downtown earlier,
vibrations were felt in the surrounding suburbia.
It, from beneath, had started to make its presence felt.
Moments later, sudden terrifying, undulating shock waves
from the bowels of the earthquake,
surged beneath the earth's crust
like a demented, mutant snake,
causing the ground to violently shake.
The rock of the offshore Fault abruptly split apart,
as the plates beneath the land and under the sea,

unleashed their grip on each other simultaneously.
Then they shifted in opposite directions,
one to the north, the other to the south, without redemption.
The ultimate, ruinous force to be reckoned with,
raged towards its vulnerable, defenceless victim
at relentless speed, in a disastrous spree.
It was a furious vortex devouring all in its path,
causing monumental destruction in its wake,
no prisoners would it take.
The behemoth was hell-bent on its own destruction,
as if it dismissed the tragedy with satisfaction.
It struck with wild velocity and swiftness,
pavements began to rise and crest,
before falling back into their troughs again.
It had surged across the city like Godzilla's monstrous hand
sweeping books off a table.
Blocks of towering buildings were rocking and swaying,
like willow trees in a rampant hurricane.
The quake laid down a quilt of devastation,
scattering debris tainted with dust-bitten breath.
Structures subsided, collapsed, crumbled like pastry,
the overwhelming deluge caused a carnage of death.
Walls came tumbling down, avalanching into the streets,
trees were uprooted, small stores disintegrated.
Chasms opened and closed, some filling with groundwater
and spilling into drains and gutters.
Chimneys, originally constructed with no earthquake in mind, shud-
dered, then fractured, toppled and fell through roofs
and buildings and onto the ground,
that was already clogged with debris and rubble around.
Brick, mortar and timber were never meant to withstand
such an onslaught on their terra firma land.
Windows shattered in showers of thousands of jagged shards,
multi-storey buildings collapsed in a horrendous crash,
that sounded like a battlefield cannon barrage.
Front walls of apartments detached themselves
from the rest of their buildings and cascaded down
in a flood of rubble onto the ground,
which crushed everything it found.

Furniture danced about as if possessed by crazed demons.
Other buildings still had their exterior walls intact,
their interiors were devastated, floors having collapsed,
beams ruptured, furniture and the inhabitants
ending up crushed in the basements.
Humans walking the pavements were felled,
smashed to pulp, under tons of falling bricks and masonry.
Wooden structures leaned drunkenly in all directions
twisted on their unstable foundations,
others collapsed in piles of splintered timber;
there were no exceptions.
The large city hall, once an impressive edifice,
had been smashed and destroyed,
its cast iron columns lying shattered in the street.
Cinemas and theatres would never reel a film
or put on a stage show again.
Their final curtain had come down.
Paper rained down like confetti,
the rails of streetcars and cable cars
were twisted and bent like strands of spaghetti.
Some of the cable rails snaked in a slow
meandering silver stream to the streets below.
Vehicles lay twisted and distorted,
over, under, sideways down,
as if they had been trampled on the ground,
by giant, metallic, martian fighting machines,
enacting out war of the underworlds.
The mains water system had been smashed,
and water was bubbling out, like springs.
Hundreds of electrical poles had toppled,
their high tension wires snapping apart,
and were whipping back like desert sidewinders.
At the same time, pipes carrying the city's gas supply,
had split apart and were unleashing their deadly fumes.
Storage tanks, in the basements of manufacturing plants,
holding kerosene and fuel oil were damaged,
and the contents were flowing towards the fiery arcs,
thrown from the electrical wires where they met
and burst in an explosion of orange flames.

Within minutes, the city would be blanketed by smoke
from fires erupting and would consume many days
and hundreds of lives before they were extinguished and
contained.
The noise, panic and bedlam was frightening and deafening,
with people shouting, screaming, wailing, crying,
their lives threatening,
as buildings in and around them rumbled and shook
in a series of convulsions before collapsing overtook.
The weirdest kind of snow
from the billowing clouds of smoke and dust,
clothed the city in unbefitting apparel.
The alighting dust was so infinitesimal,
seeking orphaned pieces of wreckage
in a voluminous burial of mounds of rubble.
After the monster had left its calling card,
all that remained was a shambolic chaos, a catastrophe,
that had caused great damage and loss of humanity.
Those who had survived were frozen in stunned shock
and silence, unable to speak or converse in whispers.
Their world had been turned into a nightmarish hell
that went far beyond imagination and justification.
Never before in the history of natural disasters
or acts of God had destruction and devastation
been so indiscriminate and so colossal.
Such a widescale disaster from violent shocks
that lasted only a minute before diminishing,
although small aftershocks continued on and off
for several days before ceasing.
All that was left of a once-thriving major city
of skyscrapers, office blocks, apartment buildings,
banks, stores, was now a hundred square miles
of jagged mounds of shattered masonry, splintered wood,
twisted metal and iron.
Armies of survivors crowded in the middle of nowhere city
and were strangely subdued. They were alive
but not knowing what to do next or where to go.
As they surveyed the desolation, they seemed
to have adopted the notion, possibility, fear,

that the evil earth monster was formidable
and might, would, strike again.
There were many people still attired in their nightclothes.
Mothers cuddled crying and bemused young children
or clutched babies, while the men discussed among themselves,
studying the damage to their homes, the scenes
of the monster's crime.
A lull settled over the ruined, frightened city.
The clouds of dust, which hung tenaciously over the devastation,
slowly dissipated and were carried away by the offshore breeze.
Cries of help from those who were injured, trapped
under the fallen structures, seeped out as muffled wails.
The city awoke the following dawn,
to an aftermath that had been unforgettably borne.
It was a wilderness of ruins, ashes and death.
The fires, which merged from small to large
had begun to dwindle.
Where flames had been, there were now streams
and palls of smoke which reached for the sky,
towards the brightening dawn.
The countless ruins of shattered buildings,
stood out, gaunt, terrible and ghost-like
in the pitiless light of the day.
The mourning, morning sun looked sadly down,
on the deafening sound of silence drifting around,
and it, from beneath, was sleeping peaceful and sound.

                    Malcolm Benjamin, Great Clacton, Essex

THE BOAT, 1950

There was something funny going on down on the River Eye,
And what was to take place there would be enough to make any
old salt of the sea sigh ...

... During the long school holidays of summertime, three sets
of idle hands needed something to do,
So three small boys among themselves bounced ideas about for
a day or two.

And after a while the three came up with a plan they all could set their minds to,
To build a boat to sail on the River Eye and each one to be a member of the crew.

They started to build their boat in an old garden shed,
Building it out of some old Brooke Bond tea chests they painted red;
Using bits of scrap timber, a few odd screws and a mixture of nails,
An old bedsheet dyed blue to be used for the sail.
They found a length of 2in x 2in timber that would be ideal for the mast,
And a length of clothesline for mooring the boat fast;
A couple of pieces of old banister rail were sawn down for the oars,
And a gangplank cut from an odd piece of wood found behind the shed door.

They sealed the boat's joints using a black pitch they found in an old tin can,
And just in case of a need to bale out was acquired a rusty old saucepan.
Then dawned the day the boat was finished and all the banging had ceased,
And for a short time there descended on the shed an aura of peace.
To the three boys the boat they had crafted was a tall ship, the River Eye the seven seas,
And from the anchor of the land, a sail brimmed with wind would soon set them free.
On the river they planned to sail around an island where swans built their nests,
And the boys' imagination was running riot with dreams of pirates and buried treasure chests.

The name they had given the boat was the *Blue Sky*,
And the day had arrived for its maiden voyage on the River Eye;
The three pals hauled the boat to the river over the distance of a mile,
Transporting the boat on a four-wheeled truck to the river in style.

The route took them down a lane that ran alongside the old

Scalford Brook,
And dozens of children fishing dropped their rods and came
running to take a look.
Word soon got around and the number of sightseers down by
the river started to grow,
And just like the Pied Piper the boat with its crew of three ended
up with dozens of children in tow.

Then at last they arrived to a section of river that would act as a
pier,
Where the deeps of the Eye rested against a dry concrete weir;
There were many willing hands to help lift the boat off the truck,
And as they slid the boat into the water, the whole operation was
observed by a flock of curious mallard ducks.
Safely moored at last by the river's bank,
Ready for boarding was laid down the boat's gangplank.
There were children of all ages standing watching from the river-
bank,
As the three boarded the boat, precariously balancing along the
gangplank.
Then, as the three climbed aboard, adjusting to its new-found
weight the boat in the water sank lower,
And the thought on the crew's minds was to prove to those on the
bank
watching, this boat was going to be a bit of a goer!

Once on board they stored away all of their gear,
And from the side of the craft the gangplank was lifted clear;
The boat freed from her moorings, to the centre of the river they
started to row,
And raised her sail to catch the breeze that started to blow;
And as all the other children gathered along the bank of the river to
watch the show,
The breeze a little stronger began to grow.

Steering the boat along the deeps of the River Eye, their sail filled
with wind the boat began to plough a wake,
The *Blue Sky* on her maiden voyage and a lot of pride at stake;
But the dreams of the three pals were somewhat about to come

unstuck,
As it started to rain and the wind squall-like suddenly struck.
The onlookers on the bank from the rain ran for cover under some trees,
And what was about to happen to the boat next they all had a good view to see.

When the squall hit the sail it rattled and shook,
And the mast creaked and groaned from the force it took;
While attempting to save the sail the scrambling about caused the boat to yaw,
And it was at this moment that one of the crew lost an oar,
The helmsman tripped and fell against the rudder,
That under the impact broke and caused the rear of the craft to shudder,
At this time a couple of joints on the tea-chest's hull began to give way,
And the boat without steerage had now begun to lose all headway.

Through one of the weakened joints on the hull, water started to pour,
And in the panic that followed someone's foot went through the hull's waterlogged floor.
Then as the boat began to list, to their dismay they lost the last remaining oar,
And it was at this time one thought on their minds was to quickly get back to shore.
With the old saucepan they tried to bale,
But gave up when the mast finally broke and they lost the sail.

And as the *Blue Sky* was listing and sinking fast,
The three decided it was time to abandon ship at last;
From the watchers on the bank there arose a cheer,
As the top of the mast into the depths of the River Eye, they watched it disappear!

So if at dusk you walk along the banks of the River Eye,
And something in the mist catches you out of the corner of your eye,

Something that from out of the mist looms, sailing silently,
hauntingly by,
It might, just might be a ghost ship on its maiden voyage, named
Blue Sky ...

Peter Morriss, Laurencekirk, Scotland

DARK POOL

Please come my friend, let's walk a while
and point our steps to yonder stile
then take ourselves by ancient oaks
to tread the way that other folks
less fortunate than you or I ...
for some have come this way to die.
Unwittingly they've hurried on
'til by yon pool were set upon
by one or more; none can reveal
but safe to say their fates were sealed.
That ancient quarry over there
now lit by sun, but be aware
its brooding pool lies black and deep
the ancient workings wide and steep.
How deep its pool, no man can say
none venture near 'ere night or day
but if they do, they scurry past
none dare to look until at last
they find their feet on holier ground
it's only then they'll look around
it's only then they'll view the scene
and bless themselves lest things unseen
should follow on, tread in their tracks
pursue them home behind their backs.

But scan the scene this glorious morn
the night has passed, its shadows gone
as swallows swoop and dive and reel
the landscape bears a goodly feel.
Bright hawthorn with their heady scent

47

bear blooms on boughs so sweetly bent
as mayflies skim o'er water's edge
and song birds nest in tree and hedge.
Those flowers of spring on every hand
as bluebells, like some merry band
of azure-headed marching men
skirt through the trees, then back again.
And primrose with their flaxen face
on bank and brae spread out apace,
gaze heavenward past cloud and sky
to charm the soul and please the eye.
On such a day it's hard to see
that evil in this world should be
around, about on every hand
intruding on the lives of man.
When shadows fall a different scene
gone are the golds, the reds, the green
replaced by changing shades of grey
to warn the stranger, *Stay away.*
An atmosphere of different hue
engulfs the land, amends the view
whilst eerie sounds offend the ear
gone is the light, the warmth, the cheer.
Why should it be that acts of men
from time to time return again?
Do acts of violence, hate, remorse
remain in buildings, trees or rocks?
Do things once felt, things so extreme
return to haunt the place, the scene
where acts of violence, thoughts unkind
might permeate another's mind?
Where persons with some special gift
might glimpse a view or catch a whiff
of something from an earlier time
a lover spurned, a dreadful crime ...
And so it was some years ago
perchance I passed this way; and so
I set my course with cheery heart
but late the hour, late was the start.

Strong were the pleas to wait 'til dawn
but pressing business urged me on
until at last with one accord
my satchel filled I stepped abroad.
I made my way unto the gate
and there beside it, sat in wait
a friendly hound, I know not whose
without a word it seemed to choose
to tag along I'm glad to say
and so we both went down the way
that we today have also trod
o'er path and track, o'er mud and sod.
The night was still, a winter's moon
to light the all-prevailing gloom
took fitful spells to thus enshroud
its presence 'neath some tiresome cloud.
How long we walked I cannot say
until somewhere along the way
quite close to yonder darkened tarn
the moon took leave, its presence gone.
I stopped, not knowing where to tread
so dark the night, so strong my dread
of walking close to yonder lake
thus not another step I'd take
until at last a moonlit glow
should guide my step, my path to show.
And when at last with beam reborn
I gazed around but was alone
my sole companion, taken flight
lost to the shadows of the night.
My disposition somewhat changed
my thoughts now strewn in disarray
should I retrace those steps I'd trod
or placing all my trust in God
should sally forth with gladsome heart
my childlike faith the darkness part
until at last with prayer and grace
I'd find myself far from this place?
This scene of haunts and ghostly yarn

that pours contempt on all who scorn.
And so it was with trembling step
with noiseless tread; as one who crept
towards that pool lest none should hear
as inch by inch I ventured near.
'Til all at once the moon shone bright
with twice or thrice its usual light
then from the lake a shade appeared
towards my side it slowly neared.
A sense of sadness so profound
filled with emotion draped around
did thus infuse the shadows' hue
I stood transfixed as if by glue
until I sank towards the soil
onto my knees as one who'd toiled
as if exhausted by the day
not fit to rise nor turn away.
To turn and flee was what I sought
try as I tried, hard though I fought
the spectre bade me to remain
relive again her hour of shame.
No longer now a silhouette
much denser than before; but yet
an eerie glow from deep within
a scowl that turned now to a grin.
With cape and gown of some refine
whilst in her arms there did'st recline
an infant clothed not for this earth
doomed to expire upon its birth.
The spectre then made haste to speak
my blood still chills; my strength grows weak
as I recall the words she spake
formed not in jest or merry jape.

I bid you listen 'fore you die
as you are now so once was I
I too was once of flesh and bone
I too once called this world my home.
I too had blood course through my veins

I too knew laughter, joy and pain
I too once knew how love could burn
I too knew hurt when love was spurned.
This child I cradle in my arms
conceived through lust and manly charms
ne'er destined to become a man
endorsed my death as if his hand
had signed a warrant by consent
as if in anger to lay vent.
Then in a fit of fearful rage
his father bade me to engage
and walk with him along this track
from which, alone, he'd journey back.
He slit my throat from side to side
in death I wear this cape to hide
the gaping wound that thus ensued
now hidden from the likes of you.
My body rests beneath this lake
with bloody throat and deathly gape
against my will I came to die
ill judgment day condemned to lie.

Though petrified, my heart felt sore
what could I do? My mind implored.
A deathlike chill sped to my soul
I shivered as if winter's cold
had taken hold of every nerve
of every sense my body served
of every sinew, organ, vein
I felt I'd never rise again
I felt I'd never leave this place
that I might too soon haunt this space.
How long I knelt no man can say
for 'twas the spirit who held sway
upon my future, or at least
until such time I'd be released
from 'neath this spell I'd knelt below
until the spirit bade me go.
And then once more the phantom spake

from deathlike trance I did awake
I knelt engrossed by every phrase
until at last allowed to raise
my frozen flesh from aching knees
the phantom issued forth this plea.

Before you part and go your way
a favour I must beg today
my weary soul now yearns release
to have the chance to sleep in peace
to have the chance to haunt no more
this quarry's dank and loathsome shore.
A man of God I do request
that he might give my spirit rest
that you might guide him to this site
that he might put these wrongs to right.

Then with a wave of ghostly hand
her presence faded from the land
as from the east a brightness slight
removed the shadows of the night.
Though weary to the point of death
with pounding heart and wilful breath
I turned for home, all business gone
still in my mind I gazed upon
that ghastly face of restless being
returned now to that world unseen
by mortal eye, lest called upon
to tell of ills and sins once done
upon this earth by evil folk
deserving of some fearful yoke
once forged in life as links of chain
'til for release their spirits strain
as did the shade I'd gazed upon
though, as the night, she too was gone.
Somehow I reached that chapel door
then once inside fell to the floor
to jar the faithful as they prayed
as anxious priests ran to my aid

to raise my head and bid me speak
though hard I tried, was much too weak
to utter words in any way
from gibbering throat as to convey
the theatre that had filled my night
and cause my being to die of fright.

Next day I led them to the scene
to where a prisoner I had been
transfixed to ground where they now stood
and promised then I never should
return unto this frightful place
lest they should find her spirit grace.
And now my friend I'll make it known
that since that day her spirit's flown
and for my part I feel at ease
that from this earth she's found release
to rest from now 'til judgment day
and hope we too might pass that way.
Should evil triumph over good?
I fear not lest those priests ne'er would
have journeyed here to put to flight
the chains that bound her here each night.

Ronnie Kilgore, Londonderry, Northern Ireland

OUR ADVOCATE

Whoever you are in this world today,
Whatever your status in life.
You may be rich in material goods,
And if lucky, free from strife.
Will you take a moment to listen to me,
As I've got a blessing to share.
It's not only for today when your life is a dream.
It's for when that's no longer there.
If it all crashed now, just where would you turn
For a helping hand or a lift.
Hear me now, my friend,

You will never look back if you take my Heavenly Gift.
I don't have money, but I have the truth
Of why this world really turns.
The purpose of man in his journey here.
In my heart this knowledge burns.
It was long ago that I learned how
To live to a Heavenly Plan,
That will never crash and let you down,
As it wasn't formed by man.
It was built on love for all human souls.
It is here for you and me
to live our lives in peace and joy
And best of all - it's free.
No matter how good we think we are,
No matter how we feel free,
This earth is ruled by God alone
His creations all are we.
We don't keep His rules,
We don't know His plan,
But it still goes on and on,
Until He says, the end is here.
No more, from mortal man.
There are conditions, you can be sure.
You wouldn't agree if not,
You being a wise one trained and honed
To discover a hidden plot,
But there is no plot, it's open and clear
In heaven there is no sin,
But being human, we err all the time
So that God can't let us in.
His laws are sure and cannot change,
Are we lost at the start, being so,
Not so, my friend, there is a way
If to Heaven we would go.
If ever man needed just one true friend
To hold his hand when he's lost,
To give him life where there's only death,
And the beauty - there is no cost.
Your bill has been paid many years ago

By suffering and pain hard to bear,
By one who gave His life for us
If the Gospel we would share,
To save our loved ones and friends so dear,
And many a stranger too, like yourself,
Do you know you are known to God
And He knows all your life story too?
You might not think you are one of His.
He created you, just like me.
He loves you too, with a perfect love.
And He wants you to know you're free,
If you take His love, if you live His way,
If you change your path right now.
You have a friend who'll speak for you
At the last moment when you can't see how
Your earthly life can get you inside
Those heavenly gates so divine,
His name is Jesus, your Lord and King
He is calling you one last time.
When the moment comes and your life is gone
And the Judgment Bar looms bright.
Jesus will be there for you
Clothed in glorious light
The Son of God, no less, will speak
To His Father on your behalf
He will plead for you, brother,
Having cleansed your sins
By His life and death on earth.
When the great God speaks, like a thundercloud
And says, *No sin can dwell in here,*
Your Friend will quietly hold you high
With eyes so pure and clear.
This man's not lost, he's tried so hard
To live a good life on earth.
I know he's sinned, it's the human fault,
But with my life and death, from birth
I bled and died so my brother could live
And enter the heavenly place,
I've paid for his sins, I set him free

So he can live by My Grace.
The Father speaks, *Enter in, my son,*
Your Saviour has bought your life
With His precious blood He spilt for you
No longer do you face death,
But eternally you'll dwell in light
In glory you'll continue on
Your deeds all blest by Jesus Christ
He's My Beloved Son.

Dorothy Gerrard, Southport, Merseyside

ISAAC AND HIS BEST FRIENDS:- A DAY EXPLORING

Isaac was a little boy
As cute as cute can be
He had two Bassett puppies
Together they made three

The three of them were ready
To explore everywhere
In the forest beyond the garden
When their mummy took them there

Even though the sun was shining
It was cool beneath the trees
The sun couldn't get through
For all the branches and the leaves

The puppies were excited
And ran off everywhere
Smelling everything they could
They thought they smelled a bear!

Isaac looked under logs
And under stones galore
And found lots of insects
Spiders, ants and many more

They came to a clearing
And his Mummy said to them
Let's have our picnic that I've packed
Then we can explore again

They ate some sandwiches
and a sausage roll or two
Had some raisins and a biscuit
And a glass of lemonade too

Refreshed, they were ready
To carry on the search
To hunt for a bear
Or maybe something worse

They heard a rustle in the trees
Oh my, what could it be?
They saw long furry ears
And four tiny little feet

A tiny nose that twitched
And a white fluffy tail
That bobbed up and down
As it ran along the trail

Oh it's just a rabbit,
Cried Isaac with surprise
I thought it was a big bear
With dark scary eyes

His Mummy said, *There are no bears*
Living in the woods
Just lots of little animals
Insects, bugs and slugs

Back home Isaac told his Daddy
As he sat upon his knee
Of all the things he'd seen and done
And then they had their tea

Tucked up in his bed
The pups sleeping on the floor
His Mummy read a bedtime story
As Isaac began to snore

Karen Walker, Whitby, North Yorkshire

FRIENDS OF ROBIN HOOD

If you need something to do,
You look around to see what's new.
Archery, now there's a thought
Could be good this target sport.

Having lessons is the thing to do,
Seeing whether it's just for you.
For a certificate you need to gain,
Until you do, maybe all in vain.

Then you'll join a local club,
Paying all the needed subs.
Coaching helps you to improve,
Soon you're off and on the move.

Now you have given it a try,
Got the bug, kiss kin goodbye.
Taking up much precious time,
Family life is undermined.

When you've grasped this archery lark,
It becomes an important part
Of your life in what you do,
Meeting friends that help you through.

With archery, your chosen sport,
You'll need strength with good support,
Protection from the mighty bow,
Can leave your arm a purple glow.

Whiplash can give you quite a nip,
The many pains, the aching hip.
All you feel are weary bones,
Perhaps one's better staying home.

In summertime you'll shoot outside ,
But when it rains, nowhere to hide,
Squelching through a muddy field,
For weaker souls there is no appeal.

When a tournament is held,
Gives one the chance to then excel.
Dressed in white and bottle-green,
You must look smart when you are seen.

When it's windy, to shoot is hard,
You can miss the inner or target card.
Arrows dip into the ground,
Covered in mud when they are found.

A field's marked out in such a way
Targets stand some feet away,
Until the judge says, *It's all clear,*
Then arrows fly right through the air.

With archers standing in a line,
Hoping that their score is fine,
Arrows land with a mighty thud,
While others lost are in the mud.

Most shoots last a single day,
Some nearby, some far away,
While others last at least a week,
So you will need a place to sleep.

So off to Dunster every June,
Some in tents, some in rooms,
Others in their caravans,
Meeting up with all the gang.

Dunster Castle, in the grounds,
Side by side are targets round.
Ready with their flying arrows,
Archers stand, both wide and narrow.

In tiny tents their gear must stow,
Behind them neatly in a row.
A telescope to check the score,
And folding chairs when feet get sore.

When all the arrows have been thrown,
And the judge's whistle has been blown,
They start to walk to retrieve their arrows,
Back and forth for several hours.

After such a tiring day,
In a field not far away,
Looking out across the sea,
You'll find them there sipping tea.

In a circle gathered round,
They sit and watch the sun go down.
A glass of wine, it may be more,
And talk of arrows and their score.

Then when its time to go to bed,
With arrows flying through their head,
They sleep and dream the night away,
And wake to shoot another day.

They also shoot in a nearby wood,
Feeling like they're Robin Hood.
Though the targets are of card,
For a passing stag it could be hard.

Just standing, watching eye to eye,
All around the arrows fly,
He thinks it best to sneak away,
Before those arrows go astray.

The week soon goes, and medals won,
Rosy cheeks in the summer sun.
Reflecting back throughout the week,
Good memories stay, 'til again they meet.

For those who work it's not so good,
To leave the scenery and Dunster Wood.
The view across to Minehead Bay,
It would be nice if they could stay.

So packing up the caravan,
Saying goodbye to all the gang,
Soon they're heading home once more,
And back to work, oh, what a bore.

But those retired, with nothing to do,
Can take their time before they move.
Then heading home in time for tea,
Reflecting back on the archery.

This will go from year to year,
Becoming good is very clear.
Medals won, experience gained,
Selected for a county game.

A sense of pride upon your face,
To win a coveted county place.
It shows just what you can achieve,
When shooting arrows is all you need.

Sometimes the weather is a pain,
Stormy clouds or too much rain.
Trying not to take a fall,
Leaves dirty clothes for them all.

Retrieving arrows from the ground,
Using a tassel to wipe them down.
They must be clean when next you shoot,
It's easy for arrows to go off route.

In wintertime you shoot inside,
No passing clouds, no need to hide.
Protected from the elements,
So one can practice for all events.

Once in a while you watch them play,
Especially on a summer's day,
When the sun is nice and warm,
You stand well back away from harm.

With a cup of tea placed in your hand,
And rules you'll never understand,
You sit and chat to everyone,
Until the match is lost or won.

This is when you get to know
Certain folk who steal the show,
Tears of laughter all the while,
Those funny traits that make you smile.

One such club that springs to mind,
These so-called characters you will find,
Down the coast towards the sea,
Robin Hood's close family.

Joan Lake, Weston-Super-Mare, Somerset

MY EDUCATION

I learned to read when I was four
and then I went to council school.
I learned the stories Homer told,
I learned of Rome and Boudicca,
though Boadicea was her name
in those old days I'm speaking of.

I learned to add, subtract and multiply,
division too, then war stepped in
so problems were a part of maths

I never learned to overcome
and decimals and fractions too
were missed along my schooling path.

I heard how Alfred burned the cakes,
I made some *asterisk* mistakes
that brought a thump upon the head
or backside beatings, enough said.
Athletics or a punishment run,
football, rugby, cricket were fun.

William the Conqueror; Agincourt;
Henry the Eighth and Good Queen Bess,
poetry; some of Shakespeare's plays
and bits of the Bible as you'd guess
I learned the contours of a map
and always to wear my old school cap.

I learned to slice a worm in half
and pin it back from side to side
to look like hull of Viking ship,
the reason why gave me the slip.
Amoeba, hydra and the frog
all featured on my science blog.

The scientists learned to make a stench,
I learned of Revolution (French),
Napoleon, Nelson, Wellington,
Russia and Prussia came into view.
I read the Scarlet Pimpernel,
The Saint and Edgar Wallace too.

The age of steam brought massive change
to agriculture, industry,
with smoking furnaces, mines and trains.
Men, women, children all enslaved,
strikes, riots, corn laws, early graves,
reform, and Britain, master of the waves.

I learned of empire and of wars
Crimea, colonies, the Boers,
and last and worst, the First World War
while brothers donned their uniforms to fight again
please not to fight in vain again
and even boy scouts had to train.

I learned a little Latin, French
and how to write plain English prose,
I played piano, learned to sing
and oh, I sang like anything.
And some of us began to find
that music thrills and helps unwind.

The years slipped by and friends were made
and somehow we just made the grade,
and then the Royal Navy called
with orders blunt, untarnished, bald.
We learned to march from morn 'til night,
to march in threes and get it right.

We carried rifles, cleaned our kit
and learned we were a shower of shit,
but all that marching made us fit
and sport brought me escape a bit -
I learned to play at any sport
that made my Navy days grow short.

I worked sometimes, but not too hard,
I learned to write a ration card,
a railway warrant and to type,
I learned to drive a Morris Eight,
to enjoy my leave and not be late,
I even went out upon a date.

And so to college for the church,
glad to leave Navy in the lurch.
Psychology, philosophy and ethics too,
Theology, Testaments Old and New,

and Hebrew 'til I gave it up.
Greek, church history with Gordon Rupp,
and football too and record scores
and a battered table tennis cup.

My education's there on view
and friends were made who still hold true
and that's the thing I'd say to you:
Although this learning's very fine,
and I'm still making learning mine,
make friends who will be true to you.

There's nothing in the world so good
as friends who are friends no matter what,
whether they are kith and kin or not.
Friends stand by you whether you rise or fall
and of all those friends the best of all
is a wife who helps a man stand tall.

Leslie Scrase, Bridport, Dorset

BOMBURST

I saw you travelling on the train
that clattered through the pouring rain
and yet I felt a shaft of sun
for I knew you were the one.

I watched you when you did alight,
I knew I had to get it right.
I couldn't bear to get rebuffed,
you might have told me to get stuffed.

But this I doubt; you looked serene,
sweet and lovely, fresh and clean.
In dress, you were a fashion plate
oh, how I longed to fix a date.

And yet fear made me hesitate

and so it was I was too late
as I started to draw near
you suddenly did disappear.

Into the tube and into the crowd
I could only sit with my head bowed
for I had lost she of my dreams
but lo, I hear a bang and screams.

Oh what a terror, it is a bomb
and yet somehow I have aplomb
to make me rush into the melee
and still the fear that's in my belly.

Into the cauldron fires of hell
I rush with others, all pell-mell
I'm looking for my dream, my vision,
not seeking fame on television.

I pass by wreckage, injured people,
a carriage stuck up like a steeple
and at the bottom, injured screaming
she of whom I have been dreaming.

I slither down, I have to reach her,
have to help her, soothe her, treat her,
for I can see that she is frightened,
that is a fear I must see lightened.

At last I reach her, hold her hand,
but find she's trapped by a steel band.
I see she's injured, badly too
Oh whatever can I do?

And then I see a steel pole near
and with a strength given by fear
I lift and strain and set her free,
she does need help, but there's only me.

I very gently lift her out
and for an ambulance I shout,
at last a fireman reaches me
and very soon she's really free.

Out of the tube and onto the street
at last, here come the pounding feet
of an ambulance crew, intent to save
a gang of men so very brave.

Into the ambulance she slides
as into the future my thoughts glide,
Can I find her? Will she live?
For I have my all to give.

My all to give, if she will have me
for I know the future can be
full of love and joy and pride
if she will become my bride.

At last I find where she's been taken,
see her, so she's not forsaken,
find she's slowly coming round
though with bandages she's bound.

As time goes by, she slowly mends,
it seems she has no other friends.
I tell her how I saw her first,
before that terrible bomburst.

I tell her it was love at first sight
and now she's going to be alright,
of how I found her in the wreck
and how she's beaten death, by heck.

And to my joy she answers me
and says, she thinks, perhaps, maybe
we were meant to be as one
and find a life that's full of fun.

A life that will defeat the wreckers
who treat life like a game of checkers
for we shall live a life that's true
just you for me and me for you.

Richard Land, Colyton, Devon

MY SOULMATE

My love bloomed like a flower every time I saw him,
It was just like I had teardrops in my eyes, on my face.
I used to spend so many happy times
Just waiting for him to come home from work,
For the man I love to come home, throw open the door.
We spent so many romantic times in the summer house,
He had his own summer beach house with his own beach.
We used to go on day trips, we used to hide in the secret
Beach house together, hiding ourselves away.
It was like a dream come true.
We could walk together along the beach
Every time I saw him we used to watch the sun rise
Up in the sky, just talking to each other.
All the time I spent with him, just looking up at the sky,
The sunrises were so magical,
Filled with mixed bright colours,
We both dreamt it could last forever.
We'd spend so many nights, days
Getting to know each other's ways
Just talking to each other in a very special way
Planning, wishing we could be together always.
We talked for hours upon hours about
How he wished I didn't have to go back home again.
So many weeks had passed when I used to come back
Home from work, I couldn't stop thinking of him
Every night I smelt the flowers that he'd send me every week
I kept thinking of all the times we were together
I wish he was with me all the time.
It was a romantic feeling,
I used to turn my lights out,

Light my candles around the room,
Light them up one by one.
I would get my beloved books and read them
Before going to bed in the middle of the night.
I dreamt of being with him and thinking about him
All the time, before falling asleep in my bed.
I used to wake up and just wonder sometimes
If I would ever see him again,
Or if he would ever want to see me.
Many months did pass, I saw him again
I made up my mind to get a job near to him,
So we could both live in the beach house together.
I sold my house to be with the man I love
So every morning I get up beside him
Smell the lovely flowers, the fresh air
Before I get ready to go to work.
I kiss him goodbye, every morning,
Tell him I love him and will see him later.
I come home, I cook him his dinner,
I am happy now we are together again.
Now I can look back on my life with a different meaning.
Love comes when you least expect it
You can find your soulmate out there
And fall in love with them too.

Sandra Goddard, Kingston, Surrey

LIFE

You have given me this book,
People with hearts that never took
Message to you, thank you.
For many people have nowhere to stay
Real people on the streets
Life has let them down, they have cold feet.
They just sit there, they have given up
Just waiting for some luck.
But that will only come from me and you
Not money, it makes them blue.

They need love and hope, a bed and to eat
They won't get that while living on the streets,
Probably richer than you at some point.
They did have a crown for they were born
Maybe someone stole it, lost or torn
Where are they now on the streets with nothing to eat?
Where are those devils, the ones we do catch
Tucked up in bed, oh they have a latch
Throw them out, not on the streets, maybe front line
Watch them get cold feet.
That cannot happen, I hear you say
Why not? It was them who put them there in the first place.
I'm talking really evil people who cannot change
For they are that way.
Everyone deserves a second chance at humanity
Third, forth, they will not change who they are.
They're bred that way.
We are all imprisoned too,
People with homes, like me and you
Nobody listens, they never do.
What do you want from society? You pay taxes too.
Messages, they're all over the show
What are they saying, do you know?
Read them and read them again
Anything from poster, photo or pen
Here on your phone, computers too
What are they saying to you?
Discount here, discount there,
Why do they have so much money to spare?
Give a little to take the whole pack,
Are you still on my track?
You travel in your car to save money,
You travel for false economy.
Wake up and think, are you giving your cards away?
Got the message?
Good.
Now you're listening and I'm glad
From shops to houses this is bad.
Only pay what you can afford

Not enough money? Then walk through the door
Rich or poor, *What rich?* I hear you say
Yes, they get slapped too, but in a different way.
Not mega rich, they don't know what life is about
They have money and power to pull them out.
You put photos of loved ones up around the town
Who have died, you hang them out with pride.
You are saying, enough is enough
Do they listen? No, they catch a bus.
For the devil does not want to see
Same old story, health and safety,
It might upset the public and young ones too,
We hear them say.
But young children must learn the world of today
Teach them the truth, they must know
Or you will see their photo.
Prevention is always better than a cure
For these are God's messages letting us know
Far too many stealing God's show,
What is the difference, do you know?
Adverts make money, faces just glow
People have to look as they pass by
That's why they do it, to catch your eye
They choose what you see,
A dead child face while you're drinking your tea!
Why not? If it happened in that spot
Messages are out there for you to read
If God had His way they wouldn't be advertising greed.
It would be the people's needs.
It's up to you all this information you have read
Is it in your heart or just your head?
Use your vote, it's up to you
Things must change from being blue
We must get back on track
The people are down, the country is flat
Maybe God has had enough too
Too much greed, no love coming through.
You're not alone, they must listen at the top
They must learn it has to stop

Millions found for Haiti, that's great, okay
But why does it take a disaster?
We could help before that dreadful day.
Yes, maybe God's had enough
He woke them up.

Lorraine Chantell Williams, Radcliffe, Greater Manchester

SEA WAKE

Along the shoreline
footprints were her only companion,
somewhere to her right
the sea whispered news
as it crept up the beach.
But all was invisible,
shrouded in the sea mist,
and her trudging form
wove and re-wove it round her,
softer than finest cashmere,
a silkworm forming its cocoon.
Her tongue explored her lips,
tasting the salty droplets
being smoothed on her face.
The dark shininess of her coat
was like a seal's pelt,
as if she too was a part
absorbed into her surroundings.
A rock loomed, and she rested,
knees drawn up to her chest,
uncovered hands seeking the warmth
crossed beneath her armpits.
Behind her the cloying sympathy,
well meant endless cups of tea,
the useless shoulder patting
and murmured repeated platitudes.
Oh yes, he was too young to go,
but the sea is a harsh employer,
and the storm had been exceptional.

Yes, perhaps they should have turned,
come back with nothing to pay the rent,
and he should not have ventured
to fix a flying rope end.
Their marriage was so new,
though they as children grew together,
but each came from fishing roots
and knew what lay ahead.
Here, where they had wandered together
she could feel him close.
As the tide reached her boulder
she imagined one tiny drop
might hold an essence still of him.
The wind rose and drove the mist away,
she too drifted home to loneliness.

Di Bagshawe, Poole, Dorset

MY SONS

So long ago when you were just a babe
Cradled in my arms so peacefully.
I felt that Heaven was near in your sweet face,
A joy to see, to hold, to love so tenderly.
I began to feel the wonder of each day,
And learn your ways, each one a pure delight.
To see the well-formed likeness growing clear.
I felt my life fulfilled, everything right.
And as you grew, your mind so clear and free,
The why and wherefore tripping off your tongue.
I watched with pride the man you were to be,
And prayed and hoped and loved to make you strong.
Full grown, you stand a man at last, cut free,
From nurturing arms of love that kept you safe
And shielded you from harm. What now, my son,
Which way are you to move?
My heart is anxious for your future bright beckons
With a glitter not quite real, will you believe, give in,
Stand up or fight, will you remember words from youth,

Or feel, will you remember honour, bright and true,
Love's forgiving gaze, will you feel safe
As each day starts anew, will you stride confident and sure
On troubled days? If I could live and bear your burdens now
That surely will appear, as always do,
But no, a man must take his place alone,
While I must pray and hope and endlessly pursue
A lonely path, devoid of purpose now,
My role fulfilled as planned by heaven above.
You may be free in time, in thought, in space,
But we are ever bound with bonds of love.
If you should ever need me, here am I,
On call forever, with a willing heart.
How big or small your needs, it matters not.
You know that I will always play my part
Of mother, guide, good counsellor and friend.
Throughout your life my love is always near.
And one day, when the time for you is right,
You'll understand my heart that felt the fear
Of loving someone else more than yourself,
Of wanting to create a world of love,
Of feeling every moment, so to give
Your heart, your life, all sorrows to remove.
And you will know the joy that I know now
In loving you through all eternity.
My son, my son, my love so deep and true
Is yours through life and goes on endlessly.

Dorothy Gerrard, Southport, Merseyside

ARTHUR

When Arthur fell into the lake
He was merely a boy about ten
Who roamed around fields and woods
For it was perfectly safe back then.
Of course we were warned of deep water
And told to keep well away.
But we chose to ignore the instruction

74

On that adventurous day.
We each had a book for recording
Butterflies, birds' nests and such;
And some had a net or a jamjar
But in truth we didn't catch much.
We always went close and looked at the lake
Not a little in awe of the tales.
Could it really contain lots of monsters
Eels, almost the size of whales?
He edged out along a protruding branch
To get a much closer view ...
Then the critical point was reached
When he didn't know quite what to do.
The decision was certainly made for him
With one almighty crack.
He was flung from his prone position
And splashed down onto his back.
The green weed closed above him
Whilst onlookers gasped in dismay
This wonderful, sunny adventure
Was becoming a nightmarish day.
Then he surfaced, a green slimy monster
With eyes wide open and round,
But the deep water myth was certainly gone
For his feet were firmly on ground.
He trudged home, squelching in his wellies
Dripping from head to toe,
And the awful stench of that water
Took a long, long bath to go.

Pauline Rust, Aylesbury, Buckinghamshire

LEARNING TO LIVE

I was brought up
to be a Bible-reading boy
and more - a Bible-believing boy.

It's in the book,

was Billy Graham's cry.
I never stopped to ask the reason why.

At last in middle life
from Bible and the teachings it had taught
I turned aside to freedom dearly bought.

But now that I
Had cast the Book aside
Where would I find another, better guide?

It seemed the natural thing to me
to seek in other books both old and new
and try to find me teachers who would do.

So many famous men there were
who left me cold, but also some
whose message left me with a crumb.

The years slipped by
and many a book I read,
packed all these teachings into my small head

and then at last it dawned;
the books may help, the teachers give a clue
but in the end it's life which teaches you.

I looked upon my life
both good and bad
and thought on all its parts, happy and sad.
After the passing of too many years
I learned from loved ones, friends, my wife,
the ways in which I wished to live my life.

At last my life's philosophy is clear;
I wish to be a warm and friendly man,
to do as little harm and all the good I can.

And when I fail, as fail I must,

I shall not beat myself with cords
or scourge myself with guilt-inducing words.

I'll face my imperfections as a man,
put them behind me with their pain,
and simply try to reach the good again.

Leslie Scrase, Bridport, Dorset

THE BEACH BALL

The ball rolled along the beach
Blown along by the gale
It began rolling towards the sea
And the little girl went pale

Let it go, her mother cried
I will buy you another
But the little girl wanted that ball
And shouted to her brother

I will get it for you sister dear
I can swim quite strong
You're not to go, do you hear
It won't take me very long

He then jumped into the ebbing tide
And swam towards the ball
It kept floating further out
And the boy began to call

Please help me, it's too far out
I just cannot swim anymore
The lifeboat crew were given a shout
For he was nearly at death's door

The boy was rescued from the sea
And taken safely to the shore
His sister turned to her mother and said

I don't want my ball any more

It nearly cost her brother his life
And it was a stupid thing to do
But when his sister had given it thought
She said, *My brother, I would rather have you.*

Violetta Jean Ferguson, Burnham on Sea, Somerset

BACK O' BEYOND

There's a little old house at the back o' beyond,
Half hidden by hedges and trees.
With broken down windows and tumbled down door,
And grass growing up through the holes in the floor.
With chimney-stack broken, and thatch falling through,
And cobwebs that sparkle with silvery dew.
But it's here that I creep from the everyday cares,
And sit dreaming dreams on the rickety stairs.

In my fancy are fey folk that skip round the door,
And play hide and seek in the woods.
There's a little brown squirrel and clucking hens stout,
And shy little field mice that run in and out.
There's the gay fragile butterfly taking to wing,
The hum of the bees and the skylarks to sing.
And the sun in the heavens sends down shafts of gold,
To a fantasy woodland, a mystical fold.

My food is the raspberries, blackberries, strawberries,
That grow in the tangled plot.
The apples that hang from the trees in the bower,
The plum and the pear, and the gooseberry sour.
And I drink from the stream o'er the brow of the hill,
That comes trickling down from the old water mill.
And runs through the meadow and round the rough bend,
And over the stones at the garden's end.

The foxgloves and bluebells deep down in the dell,

Seem to ring out an elfin song.
The sweet honeysuckle, the hawthorn and roses,
I gather each day into fresh fragrant posies.
And I sigh with content at the wind in the trees,
And I thank the dear Father for joys such as these.
For I find all the comfort for which my heart longs,
In that little old house at the back o' beyond.

Beryl Shepard Leece, Wallasey, Merseyside

THERE'S NO FUTURE IN POLLUTION

Pollution is the major scourge of life on Earth they say,
A blight on nature's cycle, turning night to day.
It filters through the oceans, determined to destroy,
Everything that lives therein, much that brings us joy.
While fishermen despair, with ever failing catches,
Until the day they all return with nothing in their hatches.
And people start to hunger, that once were all well-fed,
Without the fields of golden corn, without their daily bread.
As weeds invade once fertile soils and warming takes its toll,
A total devastation, that spreads from pole to pole.
A biblical apocalypse of plague and fire and storm,
No trees, no energy left on earth and nought to keep us warm.
A beauty that we once all knew, now something of the past,
Our childrens' children never see what once was there to last.

Time is running out they say, we need to take a stand,
To cut out waste, conserve what's left, to help this struggling land.
To find a way of living that nature once intended,
With intelligent decisions that see this madness ended.
To recycle and rethink our ways, to replant and restore
At least some of our forests, to what they were before.
Re-energise, revitalise, with wind and rain and sun,
Renewable alternatives? We've only just begun.
To educate, communicate and pass the message on,
To really make a difference, the world must act as one.
Other species have survived without a major fuss,
For decades and millennia, so now it's down to us.

(Except the poor old dinosaurs, who wandered vale and glen,
'T wasn't they who did the Earth, but the Earth that did for them).
Now, necessity breeds invention, or so they like to say,
Well there's never been more need of it, than in the world today.
So it's time to work together for a global resolution,
A whole brand new solution. There's no future in pollution.

June Squires, Broadstone, Dorset

A DAY TO REMEMBER

Do you remember, my darling, that wonderful day last July,
a day that we knew would be perfect, because there was just you and I?
We fancied a trip down the river, right the way down to the sea,
the wind and the sunshine caressed us, just the way you caressed me.

I said I would love you forever, our hearts would always entwine,
you said I was smooth and yet bubbly, just like a very fine wine.
We were neither so young, nor so foolish to dissemble or even pretend
that love's course always runs smoothly but we knew that it must never end.

At last we arrived at the seaside full of boats and pebbles and sand.
Just in time for a swim and a paddle, then on to our hotel - The Grand.
You were gorgeous encased in your swimsuit, a vision in scarlet and gold
and I knew as I watched you cavorting that you would never grow old.

For your beauty was ageless and timeless, the loveliest girl I had seen,
a mermaid plucked out of the water that shone iridescent and green.
We then sat and gazed at each other, our love as warm as the sun,
but would we be late for our dinner? No, back to The Grand at the run.

80

We lingered long over dinner, you in the candlelight's gleam
While I just sat and gazed at you, that cat that has stolen the cream.
Then when the dinner was over, the band struck up with a chord,
We danced all the evening together, two lovers in total accord.

As we danced to the music from Heaven, our fingers and hearts
both entwined
We knew the joy of perfection, lovers both well fed and wined.
We waltzed and we jived and we quickstepped, before the band
swung into jazz
And that's how the evening finished, with excitement and razza-
matazz.

Exhausted, excited and happy, two lovers fell into bed
A fringed and tasslled four poster, with a counterpane golden and
red.
The day had been one to remember, like all the things said and
done,
A day when two hearts together over despair and misery had won.

Richard Land, Colyton, Devon

ON SEEING THE FILM "THE BOY IN THE STRIPED PYJAMAS"

Not of his making the close confines
In contrast to loving freedom in meadow or farm.
Not so today while adult family take pains to hide or confuse
What no-one seems to know is taking place
Within walking distance of that garden
Behind the house. A house so buttoned up
A dying house with fearful servants and guards
Who spy or talk too much then disappear, to be seen no more,
Like a little boy who broke out to explore the forbidden ground.
Seeking a kindred soul and finding a boy his age in striped pyjamas
Shorn and pale with empty stomach but childlike spirit.
They grow to absorb each other's place and dream of different times
When wire is trodden down, but now one will cross to find a father
lost.
Only way was under, spade bursting through to reach a friend.

Hand in hand now through the rain, siren howls
And two small figures hurled into the chamber with crowds of the
unwanted dying,
Thoughts closeted in trust of showers to warm them from the rain.
Only a black mist like coal dust through that little chink of sky
To take their breath away in wonder and strange excitement
Or fear, hands tightly clasped together, doused to fall asleep.

Ann McNair, Verwood, Dorset

THERE'S A BRILLIANT NEW STAR IN THE UNIVERSE

There's a brilliant new star in the sky,
it's been here a while so clear and bright.
There she is in crushed blue velvet,
smiling and happy travelling
across aeons in a lifetime of memories.
She's calm and peaceful now.
Did you know she was a skater?
Did you see her joy as she came to a halt?
Flushed and young - a newcomer
like a magnificent shooting star.
It's not the end, but clearly the beginning
of something new.

Before long in '88 my mother appeared
at the top of a shining staircase,
Cecil B de Mille style with laughter
in her gentle eyes,
wearing an elegant grass-green gown
she knew that she'd arrived.
To be a seagull was her choice,
floating on a gentle breeze.
Free travel and magnificent views
above, perhaps I'll be the same.
What an adventure to start again
the soul has all the freedom it could desire.

We are not left behind. Death is not fearful.

Like most things it isn't quite what you expect,
it is actually a perfection of organisation
with nothing left to chance.

Pamela Davies, Bournemouth, Dorset

MARSTON MOOR

July the second, sixteen forty four
East of Harrogate and west of York
Two armies stand off on Marston Moor
Forty thousand men with death to hawk

Royalist, Roundhead and Scot, all British sons
With pike and musket and the horse
And the lurking menace of fifty guns
Ready for the day to take its course

Prince Rupert and Cromwell are both there
With the yeoman, pauper and the glover
Sharing the chill in the summer air
No scope to leave, nowhere for cover

Fearfully he stands on the cusp of this battle
His pike butt resting upon foreign ground
Too anxious to join in the swaggering prattle
Only dark thoughts in his head to be found

No give or take as hour follows hour
Each sapping minute more courage shorn
The acrid air sickly, sweaty and sour
And a darkening sky heralds a storm

Under a squall the Roundheads choose to rouse
As their Royalist brothers are caught in a nap
With the heavens opened to pour and to douse
The Prince's men find themselves in a flap

Thundering cavalry charge on the flanks
The centre a push of pike, a clash of swords

A chaotic blood-letting amongst the ranks
A frenzied, brutal, cacophony from the hordes

Fairfax's flank is routed, few will rally
His Roundheads ousted by Goring's Northern horse
But the Prince's Cavaliers suffer a heavy tally
Battered and scattered by Cromwell's Ironside force

Surges and stands as day falls into night
Newcastle's White Coats resist to no avail
Their tenacious defiance is a futile fight
As the massed Allies inevitably prevail

The doughty Ironsides have influenced the field
Northern England now Roundhead at a bloody cost
As the defeated Royalists scatter and yield
The Prince escapes to Chester, his army lost

Supine in the mud, he'd fought his last battle
Guts exposed, his blood soaked the ground
No comfort, no care, in his death-rattle
No more thoughts in his head to be found

July the second, sixteen forty four
East of Harrogate and west of York
Four thousand dead on Marston Moor
All British sons, wiped out like chalk

Lance Barnwell, Melton Mowbray, Leicestershire

SUPERMARKET

Go into a superstore, and food beguiles the eye,
You couldn't ask for more, whatever you wish to buy.
And what impresses most of all are the colours all around,
Especially on the fruit stalls, where a rainbow of colour is found.

Red apples heaped and shining, bananas, lemons by the ton,
Yellow and bright, all lying in the displays we gaze upon.

84

Peppers; red, green and yellow, in their see-through cellophane,
Huge cooking apples just below, that the box can scarce contain.

Glossy grapes, ripe rasps to savour, strawberries in their season,
Foreign fruits of every flavour, we buy, don't need a reason.
Nearby are carrots, washed and clean, orange, crisp, loose or pack,
Curly cabbage, long green beans, tomatoes, salad, rack on rack.

Potatoes, every name and size, turnips, swedes, and podded peas,
Presented there to catch the eyes, some folk asking, *What are these?*
For now and then, never fear, there'll be something new to see,
So strange when they first appear, but heaped in trolleys there
they'll be.

Cereal packs assault the eyes with countless types of grain,
In every colour, shape and size, on both sides of the shopping lane.
Carton, packet, jar or tin, *Each containing what?* you ask,
As you lean close to read what's in ... choosing can be such a task.

Displays of bread, golden, light; buns, fresh cakes by the dozen,
Assail the senses, smell and sight, the whole department buzzing.
Then the humming freezers' beat reminds us of the mountain,
Of ice creams, and the frozen meats, more expense, but who's
counting?

Choice of cold cuts or fresh meat is in the skilled butcher's care,
For good meals they can't be beat, and nearby cheeses are fine fare.
Then aromatic coffees pull, likewise refreshing teas,
A mix of fruit drinks can't be dull, and wine ... well just two of
these.

A bag of flour won't go amiss, and some baking bits-and-bats,
A few of these, a pack of that, oh, and tinned stuff for the cat.
Whatever you may need is right there in that big store,
So much food and drink indeed, yet you'll soon go back for more.

When you get home no doubt you'll find,
There's something you have left behind.
And off you'll go, think, *What a bind,*

And with full trolley stand in line.

Elizabeth Harding, York, North Yorkshire

IN THIS THEY KEEP THEIR SHAME

Lithe green parrots
Glide so high
But never find a home
Pass through the windows
Of the minds
Of those
They've never known
A flower shows its point of view
The witness stands alone
His boyish dreams hold misty eyes
The thief that stole his own demise
Now lies in empty rooms

Rose petals lie upon a floor
Where naked feet once set
A swallow leaves
A tear behind
For those it never met
A flower stands before its peers
The judge hangs his head in shame
His adult dreams hold angry eyes
Of those who bathed within the lies
For them that had no names

A wood now stands
Where a forest once grew
The mighty deer
No longer roam
Nor look for pastures new
A flower bows its head to one
Whose time has passed away
His dying dreams hold faded eyes
Of those who know they cannot cry

In this they keep their shame

Kevin Andrews, Ashford, Kent

SKY LIGHT

As day sheds its golden mantle,
in creeps the black of night.
Yet above earthly perfumed desert air,
diamonds of God's firmament so set,
blinking as though shy, provide its light;
from a zillion miles away.

Orion lies resting, stares,
his sword and belt, glisten as one,
sure to guide, whilst others stand in rota,
with early riser Venus,
Great Bear asparkle north.

Yet, comets do surpass their glory,
and cast away its dreams of darkness.
Let earthbound weights recede
and soar one's heart within black velvet,
which finds no moon.

Stars and clusters lighten path,
for lovers in tranced embrace,
their sharpness comfort all below.
Flyers wing on continental track so true,
by night, stable and smooth as silk,
with minute spark aplenty.

Supernova as a flash will streak
and pass in silent grace.
Comes dawn to dust away our reverie,
what more we need,
when we have kissed
The Sky Light.

Maurice Sangan, Guernsey, Channel Islands

SOUL OF THE OCEAN

To them she is a body of depth that harbours the fuel of the fisher-
man's wallet
To them she is a sanctuary, a home
To them she is a strength of nature to be feared from afar
To them she is an element of necessity

Adorned with seven masks she faces us
Resting in the lap of the world
Her global arms carry adventurers to distant lands
Silver hands sculpting pebbles, crafting our coastlines
For the islands she is a bridge that binds
Mirror images of isolation ripple through her body
Sounds of the sea captured in mollusc shells
Sets a tranquil and peaceful scene
A vast keeper of secrets
Power and force beyond compare

Feel her warm Mediterranean caress upon your toes
Feel her playful charm
Feel her cool salty breath wash away yesterday's sands
Feel her rage stir in the wake of a storm

Mesmerising colours glistening on shallow shores
Tempting strangers into her lair
Together she and the moon beckon the waves
In the cool of the winter, feel the flow reverse
Rich blues and deep greens darken by the mile
From eerily still to frothing at the seams
Driven by the passions of a woman she changes her mind
As her vicious tongue lashes at the motionless rocks
From the iceberg laden waters of the Arctic to the salty shores of the
Dead Sea
She is a commander of a water army
Washing waves march and retreat
One ever-changing picture of solitude
Hear her cry the essence of freedom

She is as old as the earth she rests on
She is as fresh as a new summers day
She is at the mercy of gravity
She is a fortress untamed and serene
She is everlasting currents and tides that ebb and flow
She is a silk comfort blanket engulfing lonely lands
She is a family of seven seas
She has a soul
She is The Ocean

Pamela Foster, Northampton, Northamptonshire

PEACE

Up early each morning, with no need of a clock
At peace in the garden, he spends his time
Mowing and pruning, tending his plot.
Spring, summer, autumn, whatever the clime,
But winter has a special significance
And now it's uppermost in his mind ...
It's time for the Festival of Remembrance
And George has memories of a different kind.
It's the eleventh day of the eleventh month
When peace was declared and the battle won.
He remembers his comrades in the trenches,
The stench and the mud and the noise of the guns.
He remembers the lads who were so young
Who didn't return to their homes and loved ones.
He remembers the letters he wrote every week
Thanks for the socks, and the cakes were a treat
But when it all ended, he couldn't forget
The dismembered bodies he helped to retrieve
And his life which was spared he began to regret.
So many were lost - a tragedy indeed.

The medals he won he should now be wearing,
Marching in time with those who survived
The old familiar tunes are playing
Wreaths being laid by sisters and wives.

Each one lost in their own little world
Wondering how things could have been different
If their own had returned and a new life unfurled.
Was the end of the war so significant?

It seems that not a lot has changed.
We're still at war chasing the Taliban.
Wars in other parts still rage.
Men die, and children are orphaned.

So George just carries on with his gardening
He now finds peace in his own surroundings.
The seasons will always come and go
The sun may shine and winds may blow
But his deepest thoughts we may never know.

Joan Facey, Hoddesdon, Hertfordshire

AVEBURY

The flints are dug and knapped,
Arrow stave is smoothed and fletched,
The air is cut, the mark is hit, the hunted slain,
The beast transfixed.
The hide is stripped and the meat is razored from the bone,
And the sun sets behind the ridge.
History is what now begins.

The logs are sparked by striking stone, a flame and smoke ascend
the thatch,
Moon rises, the North Star glints, ancient stories told,
As babes in arms suckle while their mothers sing.
Young hunter listens to his elder's tales,
The bravery in the hunt, excitement of the kill,
And of the shared skills performed,
As the tribe's history passes on to him.

In a dream he sees a vision, a cultivated field of waving wheat,
A motorway and pylons with their cables stride the hill,
Cooling towers evaporate steam and factory stacks distribute filth.

The sun is hidden at its prime, the hunter grips his bow and cries,
My land, my childrens' future is a wasted desert.
The cast is set, the bones are thrown and the runes are read,
His heart is broken as he watches his history being taken.

He dies and is laid out for the crows to scavenge,
When cleansed of flesh he is buried in the chalky earth to rest,
With bow, arrow and favourite spear, a treasured bronze amulet
lying near,
With a beaker filled with beer to help him on his journey,
He is covered and is hidden as his history is forgotten.

The tourists come to view and touch the standing stones,
A ball is thrown and caught, photographs are taken.
Postcards are bought and sandwiches eaten.
Beneath them vibrations may be felt,
The telling of ancient stories, the throwing of the spear,
Setting of the snare, casting of the net, the arrow flying through the
air,
And there, hiding in the blades of grass,
Mans' long destructive history of pain and sorrow.

David Grayling, Leamington Spa. Warwickshire

THE GREAT OAK TREE

The great oak tree shook in the wind
And pulled its bark tighter round its trunk
It looked at the little forest that grew around him
And most of the trees were from his acorns
That cast across the ground to where
They would be easily found by jays and squirrels
And carry them away
And the wind shook the last of the acorns from the tree
And the tree felt the first nip in the wind of winter
And it was coming his way
And as the young saplings went back and forth
Like old drunks swaying in the wind
The oak tree's thoughts turned to the past

And knew this wind would never last
For the snow was not far away
In some great display of winter snow
Where patterns made by the oak tree
As it swayed to and fro
Waiting for the fall of a branch or two
That always happens with the weight of the snow

Peter Clayton, Coventry, West Midlands

LONELINESS

I know I'm really not alone,
That all the people I have known
Beyond the veil are close to me
In thought and heart and memory;
That friends I have in distant places
Are conjured up in friendly faces
Within my mind, and though alone,
Their voices reach me on the phone.

And yet - and yet - when darkness falls
And lonely in my own four walls
I hear the wild relentless rain
Seek entry at my window pane,
In spite of fire and books and food,
And much that ought to make life good,
In spite of health and gifts of mind,
I find it all - oh how I find
It nothing worth, no longer fair
Because no human creature's there.

No-one to smile across at me
And give that kind of company
That needs no effort whatsoever
Because our minds are tuned together.
No-one to touch and love and kiss,
Oh this is loneliness - oh this
The lack of that which makes a home,

The tangible presence, loved and known.

The rain pours down, my heart is low,
Low as the clouds, like rain tears flow.
Darkness descends and black despair,
It seems that all I love and care
About is gone away from me,
The future is a tossing sea
Of sorrow, and my little barque
A lonely pinpoint in the dark.

But passing years will soften pain,
And suffering is not in vain.
The night is dark before the dawn,
The sea is peaceful after storm,
The birds come back to sing again
And eased are all the woes of man,
His joy and pain - his moment's story
Too short in time - once glimpse of glory.

Ruth Miller, Fort William, Scotland

SONG-LINES

I was talking to an Irishman the other day
About the way I reached into another world
Sometimes when writing poetry.

He spoke of song-lines
And it flashed upon me then how things connect,
How past and present and eternity
From earliest glimmers of humanity
Were met in words, all music of so many spheres,
The echo, record of man's years,
Traced across the landscapes of our lives
And I marvelled at the point at which I stood,
Bard, priest and shaman all in one
Translating from that world to this,
In lines of song

And knew at once my place, my destiny,
Embracing my vocation
In the Celtic, Saxon, Norseness of my nation
Connecting me at once to all ethnicity,
Those lines of blood and blood's deep rhythms
Pulsing through one great heart,
In speech and dance and art
In legend, myth and story
Striving for harmony, whose key is beauty,
Writing to get it right
So that we all at last may hear
Love's old sweet song.

Philip H B Chadwick, London, Greater London

I REMEMBER

I remember, rushing round the market.
Last minute shopping for those I hold dear
Pulling my collar up against the chill in the air,
Whilst the sound of hosannas rang out everywhere
Amid cries of, *Satsumas* and, *Get your sprouts 'ere*,
Dashing through stalls of red wrapping and reindeer
Excited, hopes of a white Christmas,
Well we get lots of frosts,
But it rarely snows here

I remember his face as he caught my eye,
I stopped in my tracks,
Whilst many ignored him and hurried on by,
Huddled in a boarded shop doorway,
Draped in an old blanket that had seen better days
I remember the dirt weathered face,
Amidst faded tan of summer his pallor fading to grey
I remember, his dog a Jack Russell I think
Glanced up at his master, shivering,
A hand came from under the blanket and gathered him in

I remember his board where the words

Homeless and hungry were scrawled
I remember I watched for a while
But then he read my concern and forcing a smile
I remember his words
He said, *Lady don't worry, we'll move on in a while.*
He looked down at his hat and then back at me,
Can you spare me the price of a cup of tea?
I opened my purse and took a handful of coins,
Not checking to count but as they fell into his hat
Like the brief bells of Christmas, made a jingling noise

I remember he said,
Thank you and God bless you.
He gathered his hat and struggled to his feet,
He beckoned the dog saying, *Come on, lets go eat.*
I remember the blanket draped figure as he walked away,
I wondered had I done my good deed for the day?
Or was it the pang of guilt that I'd felt?
Had my handful of silver sent him on his way?

I remember as I tucked into my turkey and mince pies
Looking around the table at my loved ones' eyes,
I wondered where the man and his dog could be,
What sort of Christmas would his be?
Was he somewhere warm, somewhere inside?
Or wandering the street with his dog by his side?
I never saw him again but I remember

Janet S Rogers, Bournemouth, Dorset

THAT'S LIFE

As kids we'd walk to the dingle, it was just four miles away
With jam butties and a bottle of water, what fun we'd have all day
What, with hide and seek and climbing trees, there was no price to
pay
We never dreamed, in those days, that those times would slip away
But the years slipped by so stealthily until we all had grown
And I fell in love, got married, and had children of my own

I used to take them to The Otter (a pub) where we would play out-
side
Where I'd roll and tumble with them and rescue them from trees
with pride
I didn't care about those folk with their disapproving glance
Your kids are only young once, you don't get a second chance
But time stands still for no man and soon my kids were grown
Then my daughter, Lisa, had children of her own
To me, to be honest it seemed those kids were heaven sent
So armed with Calpol and plasters, paper and pens, each Saturday
we went
(For a grandad always comes prepared whatever the event)
Down to my local club where I'd think of things to do
And pretty soon the other kids wanted to join in too
That's why I ended up with a creche of kids just having fun
With the drawing and the colouring that with my grandkids I'd
begun
But now, twenty years later, the telephone doesn't ring
Still, looking back, you know what? I wouldn't change a thing

Anthony P Thomas, Warrington, Cheshire

THE APOTHEOSIS OF TIGGER THE PUSS:
A HERETICAL POEM FOR MY GRANDCHILDREN

When Tigger the puss went to Heaven
He bounded in through the gate.
He knew it was very near dinner time,
And he didn't want to be late.

He was dreading embarrassing questions
Concerning a missing rump steak,
So he nipped quickly past old St Peter,
Who wasn't completely awake.

He trotted along to Jehovah
And jumped up on to his lap.
My goodness, exclaimed the Almighty,
Now here's an affectionate chap.

The Almighty caressed little Tigger
And tickled him under the chin.
Tigger chirped and purred and got comfy,
And God felt his claws digging in.

No cats, no cats, cried St Peter,
Starting up from a blink and a nod.
Cats aren't allowed into Heaven!
Don't be so silly, said God.

You must have got that from some churchman,
I make the rules around here.
The angels just looked at each other,
Then some of them started to cheer.

Bring me some dinner for Tigger,
Said God. *He's come a long way,*
And I know that he's ever so hungry.
A cherub flew off to obey.

The angels trooped round to the dining hall,
Leaving God feeding Tigger, His cat,
And many were saying that they, too,
Would like a sweet pet such as that.

So St. Michael has drawn up a waiting list
Of angels all wanting to own
A warm, furry pussy like Tigger -
It's astonishing how the list's grown.
It's the longest that's ever been known.

Patrick O'Shaughnessy, Lincoln, Lincolnshire

WASHFIELD WEIR

Sun shining on moving water,
Ten thousand dancing mirrors dazzling the eye.
The weir aslant the river, checks the mighty flow
And all the air thrills with the thunder of the fall.

97

Along the top a smooth and shining curve,
Where water slides to plummet into breaking spray.

Do you think that we can get across? asks Robin.
Robin is just eleven, I am nearly twelve.

Slide down the bank and start inching our way forward.
Hold to the lip as water beats against our arms.
Cling to the rocky bed with naked toes,
Whilst dangling shoes about our necks nigh touch the surface.

Slowly, slowly, hold tight, make no mistakes.
Seen from the bank, the weir, but thirty yards across,
Now proves to be at least a hundred feet.
Hot sun striking our shoulders and our backs,
Cold hands and arms shimmer beneath the dragging current,
All other sounds drowned by the roaring of the water.

Now the water deepens, tugging our hanging shoes.
Uncertain pause, look back - it's shorter to keep going.
With all our strength we fight the last few yards
And clinging to the spray-wet rocks, escape the tumbling water.

Mounting the bank, we flop amongst the warm dry grasses
And chirping crickets sing about our heads.
Slowly the sun's heat banishes the coldness of the river.

Then we are up and away, both eager to explore,
A whole new land this eastern river side.
And so in time we range a good mile up the Exe,
To where a wide ford wades us back,
A ford we know, below our pool for swimming,
Daring one crossing of the weir was quite enough.

A short while later, two young girls,
Friends, from the cottages below the weir,
Tried the same crossing.
Both were swept away and drowned.
We heard the news and felt a pang of guilt.

Were the two watching when we crossed?

Mark Cory, Banstead, Surrey

POST OP COMPLICATIONS

All was fine, or so it seemed,
Life returning to normal,
The building blocks of existence,
Construction, underway;
A new start in the making,
To consign the past, to history.
Infection of the internal cavities
Now a distant memory, or so they supposed;
Reenergising of the V.I.P. Patient, in progress,
The central pumping mechanism,
Filters, tubes, essential oils,
Fluids circulating in conjunction,
All seemed well ... but,

Planning permission not sorted, consent form not signed;
Fallibilities, weaknesses within the torso;
Infrastructure crumbling, thudding, abrupt tremors.

The heavenly peace and tranquillity,
Gave way to an untimely, ungodly tumultuous grumbling;
The Fast Breeder Retractor burst its endoskeleton;
The brainchild of cranium enrichment, gone to dogs;
Had blasted its boiler into orbit.

This advented a fresh beginning, of brown liquid
Yes, in the form of chocolate,
A superstar was Bournville,
The town now emersed in thick Cadbury's
Toffee, nougat, other
We witness meltdown of unearthly type;
Choco-radiation, nougat becomes nuke-art
Fall out, fall out; call out the paramedics
We've heard of salmonella in chocolate

Underground silos, tunnel networks,
Chocolate terrorism being hatched, five minutes
To midnight, to armageddon, ground zero.

Mars, Snickers, chunker busters launched
Now a real old nine eleven, choc blot, on the landscape.

Steven Bown, Chesterfield, Derbyshire

KISS FOR A PRINCE

The Abbey bells ring out once more
romance in its song.
For a prince who stands in waiting
to seal love's eternal bond.
So bold he stands, so handsome
dressed in red and gold attire,
for a love that breaks the nation's heart
to set its soul on fire.
So elegant she walks, such beauty, so grand.
As she takes the steps to reach her prince
tightly grasping father's hand.
Her dress adorned with ivory silk,
French and English lace.
A diamond tiara from the Queen
Holds her headdress in place.
A bouquet of flowers held in her hand
an emblem of past and present to be,
Sweet William, Myrtle, Lily Of The Valley
Signifies the love I have for thee.
The prince utters words to Catherine
You look beautiful, he said.
She turns and looks with a radiant smile
as he takes her hand to wed.
There were vows to take and vows to make
in the heart of the Abbey I do take.
The nation cheers, the bells ring out,
the carriage awaits as the sun shines down.
A smile, a wave for all the crowd

a kiss for a prince, not once but twice,
is where cupid played its part,
but the arrows of love from the bow that was fired
came straight from his mother's heart.
It's a love that brought a melody
to every heartbeat,
and for Catherine, a soulmate to William
a beautiful vision complete.

Rosemarie Lynn Foulkes, Mancot, Wales

THE BATHROOM SPIDER

While in the shower I did see
what looked like a tarantula looking at me.
With pincers wide open ready to bite,
that really gave me an awful fright.
But my specsavers I didn't have on
and out of the shower I was ready to run.
I tried to stamp on it instead,
that was when I banged my head.
Now the shower head it was off, hitting my toes,
landing in the trough.
Out of the shower fast I came, the spider followed,
the one I'd tried to maim.
It looked like two legs it had lost,
so over it I thought I bossed.
Blood streaming from my toe and head,
that spider I'll kill, make sure it's dead.
As it raced across the bathroom floor, with only four legs
I'll catch it for sure.
Still spec-less, a hairbrush my hand found,
whilst knocking my specs onto the ground.
As I stepped on them, my foot I slashed,
but kept after the spider unabashed.
One clout with the brush the spider I swiped, missing by a mile,
the spider looked to smile.
The bath tap left the pipe with my blow,
smashing onto my other toe.

But I'd got him frightened, he was having eggs,
then I noticed he was sprouting more legs.
Ten he had got where before only four, still lashing with the brush,
I was sure to score.
As I fell into the bath, my back to bruise,
my quarry used his one last ruse.
To the ceiling he scurried, twelve legs going fast,
that's when out of the world I passed.
I came round quickly as the bath overflowed,
not letting anything get in my road.
Out I scrambled onto the floor
which was covered in water, my blood and my gore.
The spider forgotten, an ambulance I needed,
after dialling 999 to me the paramedics speeded.
Smashing down the door with one blow,
they succeeded.
After three weeks in emergency ward ten
my injuries healing, they said, *Don't do it again.*
Now into my new bathroom in my wheelchair I roll,
it cost a lot more than you get on the dole.
Regretting hunting the spider in the end, because now that tiny spider
has become my best friend.

Terry Bednall, Pontefract, West Yorkshire

SERENITY IN TIME

I wake to watch the sunrise
Light up the world before my eyes
Mother Earth sparkles in the morning mist
By the early morning dew
She has been kissed
I take a walk upon the shore
There is rapture in the ocean's roar
I stand beside a waterfall
Feeling humbled by it all
I lay beside a babbling stream
Here I am allowed to dream

A dragonfly hovers by
Like a jewel in the sky
I walk through a forest glade
Carpets of bluebells in its shade
There's a symphony in the breeze
As it rustles through the trees
The mountains in the majesty
Towering over an azure sea
The power in a thunderstorm
The magic when a rainbow forms
I see silver in the raindrops
As they fall from out of the sky
Why did I never see before?
I will always wonder why
I see mystery in the sky at night
The moon and stars, God's heavenly light
All before me is sublime
A moment of serenity in time
Tomorrow is promised to no man
Let's stop a while whilst we can
I gaze in wonder and I pray
If God should grant me one more day
I will stop along the way

Edna Glew, Barrow in Furness, Cumbria

FAMILY LIFE

Looking back to distant days
On my parents' lovely ways
Mother, father gave us life
Married young, man and wife
Both of them born on a farm
Some bad days, others calm
Working hard and very winning
For a penny, sometimes a shilling

The Great War came with all its might
Many joined to take up the fight

Father driving up to the trenches
Bringing back soldiers on makeshift benches
A lot lost limbs, some were blind
Many dead left behind
My uncle fighting knee deep in water
Then was gassed, his health did falter

Mother's wartime service town
Her monthly income half a crown
Giant zeppelin overhead one day
Blocked out the light so they say
Up in the sky so it spied
No bombs dropped, no-one died
Wartime came to sudden end
Back together no money to spend

Life forever full of bliss
Often cuddle then a kiss
Children arrived it could be four
Then it grew to more and more
We still think of pretty Jean
Grew to be a beauty queen
In later years five have gone
Four boys left to carry on

Such a grand life we had
In old cottage always fed
From a very early age we played
Out in the fields and often stayed
To the river with fishing rod
Nothing caught, back home we plod
Out in the grain at harvest time
Running rabbits caught, it's mine

In the wintertime, sledge at night
Moving like a bird in flight
Out in the snow very cold
Never flinching, four so bold
All the family in church choir

Singing loud to reach the spire
Looking back to long lost days
On our parents' lovely ways

George Sutton, Cleobury Mortimer, Shropshire

ANOTHER CHORE

Yes it had to be done!
The loft had to be cleared.
A daunting task.
Will I find fragments of my life,
Hidden away, nearly forgotten?
I wonder.
Down come the ladders, up I go.
Boxes and boxes neatly labelled everywhere.
Where has the time gone?
The years simply roll away.
The old Singer sewing machine, the tailor's dummy,
Button boxes, reels of thread, pins and needles.
Now the boxes.
Beautiful glasses, vases, trinkets,
All manner of plates,
Very very old china wrapped carefully in old newspapers,
I read some of the headlines and smile.
Clothes outdated, nearly new, some old,
Hats. Shoes and more shoes.
Off to the charity shops in bags.
Now the photo albums,
Memories flood in.
Camping days, three girls and a spotty dog.
Your eyes fill with tears.
Pressed flowers collected in the hedgerows and on the downs.
Black and white prints.
Dearly loved family. Nearest and dearest friends, no longer with us,
People and places,
A story in itself.
Birthday cards, Christmas cards, anniversary cards all there,
Out these must go.

Thankfully memories live forever.
Wow, the old dressing up gear for New Year's Eve,
Flimsy underwear, scarves of all colours, wigs,
Old records,
Simple, clean fun, laughs and giggles all around,
Happy days.
Task completed. Hatch now closed.
No more hoarding,
Except for pieces that are simply treasures beyond gold.

Betsy Tench, Throckley, Tyne and Wear

METRIC FEVER

Oh, the dreaded metrication,
Has arrived to stay forever,
I never learnt of this at school,
And I'm still not very clever.

No doubt, the clever politicians thought,
It would be quite amusing,
To be like French and German folks,
But I find it most confusing.

Pounds and ounces I understand,
Now it's kilos and grammes everywhere,
But how many grammes in an ounce? I don't know,
And I'm old enough now not to care.

I learnt of gallons and quarts at school,
Now there's petrol and milk in litres,
And vital statistics are vital no more,
For they're measured in centimetres.

They say that soon they'll have to change,
They way they sell beer and stout,
It won't be sold in pints anymore,
But half litres and we'll all lose out.

In pounds and ounces I've always worked,
Following my old recipe books,
But the new books now have metric weights,
So it hasn't been kind to cooks.

I always knew my size of shoe,
Was a good broad-fitting eight,
But they told me in the shoe shop,
I was not conversant and should get up to date.

The lady looking at my feet,
Said, *It's very plain to me,*
The shoes you need to fit those feet,
Are a size number forty three.

And now my old thermometer is also out of date,
But the weathermen on telly say everything is great,
They say degrees in celsius without any further doubt,
Can be converted easily, but I can't work it out.

I shall work in pints and gallons,
As I do not like the litre,
And prefer old feet and inches,
To the dreaded Euro metre.

And those faceless men in Brussels,
If they could have their way,
Would have kilometres on road signs,
But I hope that's miles away.

John Parry, Brecon, Wales

BAD HAIR DAY

I hadn't seen her before on the bus,
Sitting quietly, anonymous.
On her own, eating a Twix,
In front of me on the 876.
Then she started, scratch, scratch, scratch,

Her fingers deep in the mousy thatch.

I saw her now, hand on top,
When was that scratching going to stop?
Mesmerised by the scraping beat,
I pushed right back into my seat,
Scared if the nits could jump the gap,
I itched to give her hand a smack.

Her coat was black, showing the fluff,
On shoulders covered in hair and dandruff.
Had she got out of bed in a rush?
When did she last use a hairbrush,
To gather back those unruly strands
Into that reluctant elastic band?

Still she scratched, hardly stopping,
By now, I know, my eyes were popping.
Anticipating horror, shock,
Would I see the actual livestock?
Praying if I did, then she,
Would get off the bus long before me.

At last she stopped and I heaved a sigh.
I tried to read but found that I
Could not help looking over
At that messy white-flecked collar.
Then I lifted my hand, poised my finger,
Here was my stop, I was out of danger!

Edith Anderson, Shirehampton, Avon

THE TRAVELLER

We hear a piece of music and travel back in time,
To the place we store our memories, a snatch of the sublime.
Transported in an instance. In the twinkling of an eye.
To a place from that secret compartment, soft beauty, white sands
and blue sky.

Paris in the springtime is a beautiful place,
Where lovers find love one more time.
Monsieur and Madam eat their freshly baked bread
And bask in that wonderful clime.

What of Morocco with its sights and smells.
All the colours, a feast for the eye.
Fabrics and spices are found in the souks
All arrayed to tempt you to buy.

Egypt is truly a wonder,
With pyramids and temples and tombs.
Where time has stood still for thousands of years
And the world now has Tutankhamun.

So conjure up the atmosphere of the places you have been.
Taste the food and feel the sun and see what you have seen.
Re-create those wonders and holiday once more.
Travel through the tides of time all brought through memories' door.

Verna Broadhurst, Didsbury, Manchester

HAPPY NEW YEAR?

Relentlessly the clock ticks off the minutes of the year
Ahead of us the jollity of all the New Year cheer
The bells, the drinks, the fireworks, the cheery well-meant greeting
The kisses and embraces and the happy long-lost meeting
The smiling faces wishing us good health in months to come
Not knowing that this threshold simply leaves me feeling numb

Inside I cry for a father frail whose grasp on life grows weak
I cry for myself as I carry on though the future's looking bleak
I cry for my Mother holding on to the man she has loved for years
I cry for her pain as she tries to cope despite her gnawing fears

But my daughter carries a growing child with all the joy that brings
When I think of her nestled baby my fading hope takes wings
As one life ebbs another swells beneath a hopeful heart

109

A human soul arriving - another must depart

We know we all must leave this world to face the great unknown
But we fear to make this journey and travel on alone
We grow, we hope, we fail, we cry but we somehow stumble on
We carry on as best we can to meet each brand new dawn
Our frailty makes us human but faith can make us strong
And love and hope can see us through whenever things go wrong

This time of year is poignant - a time to reminisce
A time for friends and family to show love with a kiss
But as we backward cast our thoughts we also look ahead
And sometimes what we sense or know can fill us full of dread

New Year will come with good and ill - uncertainty is sure
And what we fear we cannot change - we simply must endure
I cling to thoughts of my grandchild to help my heart to mend
And silently promise my Father to be with him to the end

No matter what I'll face it all as I wipe away a tear
And try to mean it when I say, *A happy guid New Year*

Margaret Hunter, Stirling, Scotland

AN AUTUMN MORNING

On a beautiful morn in November,
When nature was quiet and still,
Four people - all wearing wellies,
Took a dog for a walk on the hill.

When we set out on this fine morning,
We weren't quite sure what we would see,
But nature wasn't as quiet as we thought,
She was busy as busy can be.

A red admiral butterfly sunning itself,
On a long grass stalk sodden with dew,
Enjoying the sun on these short autumn days,

Its wings spread out, red, white and blue.

Up from a pink Ragged Robin,
A bumble bee buzzed to the sky,
Lazily searching for pollen,
As if 'twere a day in July.

The peace and the quiet was so soothing,
Then suddenly out from the wood,
Ran a beautiful deer we had startled,
Running as fast as she could.

Rambling across a lush meadow,
When, there in the wet grass we spied,
Occasional clutches of mushrooms,
Trying their hardest to hide.

Up went a yelp from our four legged friend,
As a rabbit took flight from some kale,
She chased it some way till it went to ground,
Our last view, a white bobbing tail.

So please don't take nature for granted,
She's truly a wonderful thing,
From summer we slip in to autumn,
From winter we stroll in to spring.

Kathy Wilson, West Lavington, Wiltshire

THE SEASONS

People dream of permanent sun
But I would miss the fun
Of seeing the seasons transform
Blending and altering as they reform.

The winter though grey and pale
Still has the ability not to fail
To bring astonishment with pillowy snow

And six sided snowflakes blowing to and fro.

Then the excitement of green shoots bring
Early warning that it is nearly spring
And the delicate snowdrops come along
Before the glorious daffodils trumpet their song.

Spring a time of new life
Gives way to glorious summer days rife
With bright colours and buzzing bees
And spending time out of doors at your ease.

The nights draw in and autumn chill
Begins to bite through but spills
Into mists and a glorious show of coloured fall
Before finally succumbing to winter's call.

All four seasons have their place
The rhythms of nature at her own pace
Bringing forth all her beauty through change
For us to enjoy and wonder at her range.

Janette Patterson, Middlesex, Greater London

ONE MAN'S MEAT

Captain Murderer was of the marrying kind;
A wealthier man you'd be unlikely to find.
It made him attractive to the unmarried lady.
These he could select for their outstanding beauty
But sadly he had a merciless appetite.

He would marry them in style
A coach swiftly pulled by twelve fine horses
From nose to tail a dazzling milk white
But always with a red spot on the back
The stigma of a young bride's blood.

Once the great feasting and revelry is over

The Captain and his wife settle down to married life.
This begins with the making of a pie.
The Captain supplies a golden rolling pin
A pie-board, and a baking dish both of silver;
All the ingredients except the meat.

The wife in an inquisitive vein
Will ask the Captain, *Where's the meat?*
He will reply, *Look into the looking glass.*
She, uncomprehending of his sense of humour
Rolls out the pastry, lines the dish,
Displaying her culinary arts her only wish,
Before his sword is drawn and comes the swish
And the dull thud of a head upon the floor.
Of course, she will be tastefully arranged
So the baker's curiosity isn't inflamed.
As the Captain gnaws each bigger bone
He recalls the wives he's previously known,
How they've afforded so much pleasure.

So, young ladies, beware rich men widowed many times
Given to filing, not brushing their teeth at night.
Look for the red spot on the horses' backs!
When he points out flowers in the garden as garnish for house-lamb
You should be sensing that something's not right.
And when you see that wicked glint in his eye
It's high time you thought about making tracks;
Your mouth-watering looks would be wasted in a pie!

Tony Sainsbury,Huntingdon, Cambridgeshire

OH, WHAT A NIGHT

Retirement is approaching, a party has been mentioned
Great idea, glad rags on, ready to go.
Delicious food, delighted at seeing workmates
This will be a special night.

Band playing, feet sore with dancing, sweating, shaking body and

soul
People amassed, people I recognise
Surely they weren't here to see me?
Hello, they said, *How are you? Nice to see you again.*

Happy retirement they chorused, gift in hand
So surprised I could not speak
A bouquet of lillies and roses, fragrance supreme
How did they know my choice?

Wrapped in gold bows, beautiful in awe
Balloons waver in the breeze
How kind people are, so happy
Drinks all round, cheers.

Party bags were given, blowers, balloons and comb blowing
Illuminated bracelets, laughing and singing.
Speech was given, what kind words, I felt so humble
Never realised people felt that way.

How I treasure their friendship, they encouraged me, supported,
And truly made my job so happy.
Didn't want the night to end, truly perplexed
Wrapped in emotion.

The night has ended, memories I will treasure
On dry day's, and wet day's
I will dream of this day
Oh, what a night.

Carol Smithard, Uttoxeter, Staffordshire

LOOK BEFORE YOU LEAP

She stood there in her underwear
Not knowing what to do,
Her clothes had gone, she'd not much on ...
Knickers, bra and shoe.
Help me please, she cried in vain,

I don't know what to do,
My clothes are gone, I've not much on,
I only have one shoe.
Don't worry dear, the woman said,
There must be some mistake,
Go back and look upon the hook,
No-one your clothes would take.
As she went to look upon the hook
Her body shook with fright.
Her clothes had gone, she'd not much on ...
Not a pretty sight.
Her mind a whirl she saw a girl
Standing in her clothes.
She shouted, *Stop.* Grabbed a mop
And what do you suppose?
She chased that girl around the shop
Brandishing the mop.
Shoppers gasped as they flashed past,
So fast they couldn't stop.
They finished up in a heap
Upon the saleroom floor,
They laughed so loud they drew a crowd
Who peered in through the door.
The girl said, *What a funny thing,*
Aren't you in No. 4?
All your clothes, I do suppose,
Are hanging on the door.
So this girl she'd just chased
Wearing jeans and top,
Wore the same clothes that came
From a local shop.
Sure enough it was a fact,
Her clothes appeared in place.
A big mistake. Her knees did shake,
She blushed in sheer disgrace.
She quickly dressed in jeans and top
And found her other shoe;
She didn't hide, but rushed outside
Without much more ado.

Now there's a moral to this tale
Of landing in a heap;
Don't be in haste, no time to waste,
So look before you leap!

Patricia Barnicott, Windermere, Cumbria

THE GREAT BEWILDERMENT

Table fellowship with his Lord,
Judas, the great enigma;
Judas, the unfathomable riddle
Went out, and it was night.

Night indeed, to hasten his Master's
Grim path to gruesome Golgotha;
To bring to pass his Redeemer's
Hour of darkness,
Actuated by the basest of passions;
Thirty pieces of glittering silver,
The paltry reward for a man's transgression.

And, for a fleeting moment,
The history and fate of the world itself
Lay in the soiled hands
Of this terrible traitor,
For Satan had entered his heart,
And it was night.

Jesus, *Despised and rejected of men,*
A man of sorrows and acquainted with grief,
Betrayed and handed over, into the clutches
Of the religious Gestapo.

Now, in a frenzy of despair, and seized
With the deepest remorse
And fruitless repentance,
The great enigma hanged himself from a tree
And all his bowels gushed out

And it was night.

So, if you claim to be human,
Believe there is a God to punish or reward
All our doings here.

Jack Barnetson, Edinburgh, Scotland

PICTURES OF THE PAST

In the good old days
There were a hundred ways
No need for automation
We were there for each other
To help one another
And problems were solved without too much bother

Mrs Brown knew Mrs Jones
And all the little Joneses
They all walked to school holding hand in hand
The streets were safe for children then
To walk about or run around
The bobby on his daily beat
Was kind and helpful, nice to meet
Helmet on head, big boots on feet
He was an imposing figure

Sunday morning shops all closed
Church parade took place
People in their Sunday best
Walked to church along the streets

Then back home to Sunday roast
The best meal of the day
After which the rest of Sunday
Just passed quietly away
Making toast for tea with a toasting fork
Before an open fire

Scenes from an era short and sweet
When life was lived to a slower beat.

Grace Ball, Worthing, Sussex

THE PASSING YEARS

I can't believe another year has passed
It's my birthday once again;
I don't want to get out of bed too fast
As the mirror makes me look very plain.

I wonder if I will get a card or two
And maybe taken out to dine;
Wearing my favourite red satin dress
Which makes me look slim and fine.

Well sadly the postman didn't come
No birthday cards for me today;
I am feeling very sad and glum
Better put the satin dress away.

I will phone for a pizza to eat
And stay in and watch a film;
Well, someone might come to visit
That would make my day complete.

All my children are very busy
They have their lives to live;
The grandchildren are happy and dizzy
With sweethearts and learning to give.

Next year I will have a party
And take my family out to dine;
We will eat with appetites hearty
And drink a toast with fine wine.

Shirley Wescombe, Crawley, Sussex

CHILD OF MINE

I have to go to school today
I've just been on my holidays
It was lovely just to be
Out there in the fields and running free

My fingers are all black and green
From picking hops so many seen
Collecting wood to make a fire
I watch the flames as they leap higher

I fetch the water from the farm
The bulls locked up he cannot harm
My feet are heavy with the mud
And as I walk they make a thud

In the morning's cold and frosty mist
As God's frozen breath the new day kissed
The lorry with open back brought me here
Ice cold winds bring forth my tears

But when the morning work is done
I make the tea, I eat a bun
It's time to walk out to the woods
This part of the day is very good

As I reach for my father's hand
There is no feeling that's more grand
We walk together he and I, he tells me all the birds that fly
He tells me all the trees, he tells me of the earth
And surely in all the world there's no one with more worth

I look up at him and I can see the love that lives in him and me
Our life is sweet yet full of strife, for him I know I'd give my life
He tells me I'm his special girl, a diamond and a little pearl
And all that pain that he goes through
I'd gladly bare he knows it's true

Now back to work and Mum has baby at her breast
I rock our baby in his pram while Mum drinks tea and has a rest
I see the sun shine through the hop vines and I think this holiday
really is the best
Everything of value in this world is here in this day, this moment in
time
This is my world and this world is mine

Peggy Rolland, Guildford, Surrey

VIEW FROM A RESTAURANT WINDOW

The cars go rolling by;
You don't know where they come from or where they go,
They're in the middle of their journeys,
Some go fast, some go slow.

The buildings are a convenient backdrop;
Different architectural styles,
Most are Victorian, some are modern,
They go on for miles and miles.

Into the town or out in the country;
The cars eventually stop,
Going to work in the city,
Or going home by the shops.

The vehicles reduce in number;
The street is getting dark,
You make your way out of the restaurant
And join the people on the footpaths.

You finally get home;
Your day has been relaxed,
But the view from the restaurant window,
Just lasts and lasts.

The cars go rolling by;
You don't know where they come from or where they go,

They're in the middle of their journeys,
Some go fast, some go slow.

                    John Carr, Wolverhampton, West Midlands

KINGFISHERS

Like some joy lost overnight
Blown away in afternoons
Victims of change
Storm cock barometers
In a wild wind
Nothing special or guaranteed
Growing cold until you realise
Teasing the seed from the fruit
Heavy thunder clouds
Hoping they don't come too close
To confront, a gentle blackout
The voices and noises that can't be ignored
Denied or refused, a poem about blue light
Saturday night, flood my mind
With warm light, all this and more
But I'm sure we're still the same
Shadows under our eyes
Saintliness and sin
Nights with only the stars for company
And people who loathe and detest
Then dismiss lost souls
Guides of empty oceans
I recoil and feel nothing leave
We can't let it show
A room, a candle, a silver star
The river has run its course
Passing through the night
Dark water falling in fragments
The lake must be filled
Kingfishers, oyster catchers
The dust of the waters
Our stolen days

I suppose they're erecting monuments
But who am I to say

Bruce Martin, Dunfermline, Scotland

BELSEN SYNAGOGUE

Star of David, symbolic huts,
Waling on every wall of man's conscience;
Boots of barbed wire lead to sacrificial fire.
Trucks, mud. Curly locks, violin mocks.
Suitcase, no striped pyjamas, yet.
Yellow star, we dare not follow you,
Did they know you were a Jew? Only a few.
Wagner lover, jackboots stomp, laughs tenderly at lover's romps.
Berchestgarten love nest, *Cuckoo* reigns supreme, champagne over-
flowing,
Mountains hide the screams.
Shivering forms of David, cloth stars hang on thread
Broken constellation, dead upon the dead.
Synagogue of rotting sheds, ears frozen against the shaven heads.
Cuckoo swims in music's sea
Screams commands to military.
Patting childrens' chubby cheeks,
Kill them quickly, I hear no shrieks,
Offer them a shower today
Mutter, mutter, do you pray?
Electric barbs for Christmas Day, I love my fatherland.
The *Cuckoo's* chest with pride was swollen,
How dare they say a race be stolen,
I do it for my Ayrian stock, besides, they come in speechless flock,
Who is this God they call, this star to them be all?
My troopers tell of chanting hasty prayers as they fall,
But victory should be mine, their cloth star has no shine,
The spotlights in my camps give out more light than this dull star,
More music shall I play, to think where their strength lie?
My name will last a thousand years, the star will surely die.
Machine guns at the posts, alsation dogs the hosts
They still in floods arrive, lemmings quick to dive,

Happy to die, star eppulates high. Knowing Zion awaits,
To unlock Judah's gates.
Must return to war,
Dying Rabbi keeps score,
Counting stars, on my bunker, nearby.

Betty Fenton, Hunstanton, Norfolk

ALPHABET

A line of twenty six letters of the alphabet in a poem to behold
Betting and juggling the letters into words is a lot of balls to play
with
Can it be done with common sense? In my case I think it will be
easy
Dancing and mincing through all the words for a menu to see
Ebbed into wave upon wave of letters to be mixed about

Flying the letters and words as if upon a roundabout
Goodness me, so far so good, let's see seven lines gone in so far
Hack as I am a scribbler that forewords ahead
In other words, more notes to come to ahead
Just going forth, so far liken to building a bridge too far

Keeping respectable words thus so far so good
Landing words now liken to fish caught in a net or a website
Many words now feeling like a cow that's jumped the moon
Numb is thy hand, but to carry on is so grand
Onwards and forwards the words are going

Picking them out, so far so good
Quickly realising that I'm well over half way
Ranting and raving the words into play
So what do you all think now? Maybe mad as a hatter
To think that what I have written so far

Understanding the collections of words as seen
Valiant so far as becoming with the words
Wanting to end it all, but not many lines to go now

123

Xerox machine ready for copying my poem now
Yawning my head off, as one more line to go
Zest that I am now to finish it all

Charles Adams, Hemel Hempstead, Hertfordshire

THE BUZZ OF A MARKET

There's something about a market
That brings a buzz everywhere
For here one can find such bargains
And the browsing is beyond compare

Fresh flowers, fruit or veg, take your pick
Homemade pickles and chutney too
Records from yesterday to bring a tear
And many tools for the handyman to woo

Handbags and purses, needles and thread
Bric-a-brac galore
The chances are high that you'll come back with more
Than you actually bargained for

Clothes and slippers, plants and crafts
Wool weaving magic in the air
Books and CD's, curtains and towels
Something for all everywhere

Experience the buzz of a market
The electric atmosphere, the tang in the air
And somehow I think like me, you'll be hooked
And come back for more and more

Joan Kernick, Newton Abbott, Devon

COMMUNICATION

Let's walk and talk
We have to do it right.

Calm and quiet
No need to shout and fight.

Listen to each other
That is the only way.
Tune in to each other
Make the most of every day.

Messages to each other
Voices down the phone.
Letters through the post
So we don't feel alone.

It's nice to communicate
Discussing this and that.
Everyone can do it
It's good to do chit chat.

We all need love and friends
There's no excuse to just lose touch.
With telephones and internet
It doesn't take that much.

One talks the other listens
And then you swap it round.
And before you even know it
Another friend is found.

Open up and let it flow
Get it off your chest.
We all just need to talk
It works out for the best.

Yet no-one said it's always easy
No promise it's always fun.
Communication is the answer
The question's how you get it done.

Communication

It's written in the stars.
Communication
There's no response out there on Mars.

Communication
Even just to make amends.
Communication
Spreading joy between all friends.

Yvonne Stanley, Hawick, Scotland

MECHANICAL LOVE

I love you,
At least I think that I do.
Bring me another cup of tea,
Then I'm sure you'll agree, that I do love you.

Well, don't just stand there,
There's the shopping to do.
Don't you know?
I really do love you.

Now, why are you out there,
In the snow and the rain?
Doing the ironing on the lawn,
At this time of year, you're driving me insane.

But I do love you,
It's plain to see.
Just paint the kitchen next,
Then it will be time for tea.

And there's the laundry, please go to the laundrette.
When you've done that,
Go to the grocers,
And buy some courgettes.

Oh I do love you,

A little polish there, a little rub here.
And new fuses for you,
You know that I care.

Now, he's gone at last, what a mess I'm in.
I knew that I should not have drank,
That last glass of Saki and Gin,
On my Eastern holiday fling.

That Japanese salesman, he was so convincing,
I know that you're single, and lonely as well.
I've got something here, just for you,
Something to sell.

He'll make you so happy, just plug him in,
And keep telling him that you love him every week.
Please meet our super new model Robot ... George.
Just fifty thousand Yen, and he's all yours to keep.

Christopher Bragg, Hull, Yorkshire

DREAMS

Thank heavens for dreams that I dream every night,
For dreams are far better, even than life.
As everyone is there that I lost in the past,
And the world at my feet, all my friends at my grasp.
I do all that I want that I can't do in life,
And it goes on forever, free from all strife.
I wake when I want to and sleep while it lasts,
It's a far better life than I could ever ask.

I sleep long and deep and I snore so loud,
But who is to care when my sleep is oh so sound.
Thank heavens for sleep and dreams that are real,
It drowns all my sorrow and the hate that I feel.
For life is so cruel and hard to digest,
And with everyday life, I find it hard to rest.
So I love my bed and I love my sleep,

As only my real life makes me want to weep.

When you are poor and dream that you're rich,
Oh what a feeling, such a heavenly bliss.
Dreams are more alive than life seems to be,
Unless you have nightmares dreams are trouble free.
Thank heavens for dreams that are more real than life,
You shut out your troubles and shut out your strife.
I hope in my life that I don't stop dreaming,
As I go about life my energy is steaming.

Life is so great when you can go to bed,
You can shut out all the things you did instead.
When your body is tired and you have to rest,
You blank out your mind and think of the best.
When you wake up in the morning feeling fine,
You find some friends and go out to dine.
For this is a great life if this is the way you live,
The whole world is at your feet ready to give.

Dreams boost up your life with memories in store,
You live such a way you never have before.
When you wake up in the morning you think it's real,
Thank heavens for dreams, their real life you steal.
I hope my mind never goes blank at night,
To face life alone gives me a great fright.
In the comfort of my home I love my day,
I am so happy in my every way.

Margaret Burtenshaw-Haines, Whitland, Scotland

SPEND SPEND SPEND

Viv Nicholson, a coal miner's daughter
Won the pools in Castleford, Yorkshire
So for the first time in her life this lass
Had her hands on a large lump sum of cash
Life had been hard, on handouts she did depend
Now she shouted out loud, *I'll spend, spend, spend*

And this is what she did, she spent the lot
A detached house in Garforth, a nice little plot
A pink American Cadillac, and hair to match
This all sounds good, but what was the catch?
Well, they partied hard and lived it up
Celebrating each day, like winning the cup
But then horror struck, a terrible crash
She lost her soulmate, his car in a smash
It was all very sad, the bubble had burst
She was dying inside, as she followed the hearse
Now she was all alone, except for the kids
The thousands had gone, and now it was just quids
Her life story was made into a West End show
So what's happened to her now? You might like to know
She lives in an end terrace, just two up and down
Any spare cash and she's straight down to town
She's kept to her roots has this local girl
Life was for living and she gave it a whirl
Now she's turned to Jehovah, Jesus loves us all
She's happy now, but hey, she did have a ball.

Hazel Oliver, Castleford, West Yorkshire

INCURABLE

Faces, faces emerge from the crowd,
Developing clearer as my brain allowed,
Awaiting recognition, a sign from me,
Helping me to know who I might be,
The dreams of yesterday flood back,
When times were hard and my senses did lack,
Feelings and knowledge of what was to come,
When I could count my life as a sum,
Now all I remember is pain,
Hurting the more not knowing who to blame,
What is the reason for luck so bad,
That leaves me and others so very sad?
Count our blessings we are told,
I would, given the chance to grow old,

Free me of this burden so great,
Could it be I should have another fate?
How I dreamed of things I would like,
From childhood, like riding a bike,
To be a proud parent and cuddle my child,
Just to hold something so meek and mild,
But I now have no power even to hold my arms out straight,
They only hang down to swing like a garden gate,
I don't want pity, I want a cure,
Please someone find one and tell me you are sure,
This blurring of vision, this loss of muscle tone,
Will all disappear as miracles have shown,
I try to enjoy life, not let it go by,
But each day I breathe a heavier sigh,
Without carers I am helpless as a babe in arms,
It's their care and attention that soothes and calms,
My racked mind, my troubled heart,
If only I could have a new start,
The pictures begin again to fade,
Colours mingle, blue into jade,
The faces now blurred-over are a sea again,
It's lights out time, it's nearly ten,
The morning will come but will I wake content,
To find the cure that heaven sent?

Patricia Clark, Braintree, Essex

EVERYTHING I OWN

Screeching out for attention, crying out to be heard,
Asking people, *Are you OK?* When I have forgotten that word.
Not blaming or complaining, but stating just a fact,
Saying I love you to the mirror is staying to the pact.
Looking on at loving hugs and desire burning eyes,
If people do speak nicely it's only common lies.

I don't know anybody, I don't love any eyes,
Wondering if I stayed behind would there be any broken ties?
Don't miss anybody, apart from my own blood,

Sometimes wondering would anyone notice if I clothed myself in mud?

Drowning quietly in my loneliness, but why?
When everything I own ...
Yet objects aren't the things,
That make a house a home.

Trudging gently through the trees,
Water lapping at my knees.
Breathing deeply through my tears,
Only thinking of my fears.

But why? Just ask and gasp for breath,
But why? Just ask and touch the clouds,
Feel the softness in your touch.

And long to heal those who see the same,
To learn to love the world again.

Alicja Smith, West Moors, Dorset

I AM AN ARISTOCRAT

I am an aristocrat
To you I'm a plain old cat.
You serve me my meals
But really I'd love to steal
Your meat.

I am an aristocrat
To you I'm a plain old cat.
You groom me weekly
But really I say it cheekily
Do it daily.

I am an aristocrat
To you I'm a plain old cat.
I love my food and want more
Give in and dig into your store

Of treats.

I am an aristocrat
To you I'm a plain old cat.
To you my life may be a bore
But I do love a snooze and snore
On your best cushions.

I am an aristocrat
To you I'm a plain old cat.
You can't see
Like me
In the dark.

I am an aristocrat
To you I'm a plain old cat.
I love to hunt and chase
Mice, but you say that it's the wrong place
To leave them on your clean floor.

I am an aristocrat
To you I'm a plain old cat.
I love to be stroked and loved
But watch out if my claws become ungloved
For I scratch.

I am an aristocrat
To you I'm a plain old cat.
You are my staff
And I'll have the last laugh
For after all I am an aristocratic cat.

Patricia J Tausz, London, Greater London

LIFE IN THE DAY OF A CAT

Yes, I am that horrid ginger tom cat that humans love or hate and
moan about
Every day potting, pondering, touring, hedgerows, gardens country-

132

side nearby
Where tasty morsels conveniently hide away, listening to the birds, chatting warnings
In yonder trees avoiding my hunger pangs of needs, crouching, remaining, silently
Among foliage of cabbage leaves a starling, unaware of the dangers of my presence
Lurking in the undergrowth, still working with concentrated attention, full of activity
Relieving the ground of slugs and worms, suddenly retreats, passing limitation,
Beyond my capabilities, what went wrong?
More dissatisfaction as heading for another designation, the robin spies on me
With an evil eye and contempt while skillfully balancing on a rusty prong handle
Now resting after my high expectation of a midday snack on the old green garden
Chair that is mouldy from being left out all winter
Idealising unscrupulous thoughts that stray to next door's fish pond, where fish
In welcome skins of tantalising gold, reflecting in the sunlight rays
Of the midday glow, temptation too great, cannot renounce my evil notorious
Behaviour through tingling tense excitement, that the invited path includes
Sources of hidden danger, about to dip a paw, the thunderous disputes of wrath
Hailed from a half open door threaten disaster as objects of mass destruction
Hurtles in my direction, hoping for retaliation and refuge ... must make a quick exit
To another location, the sanctuary of the old red brick wall, where one can take
Refuge, curling in a comfortable oblivious state on the warm, sunny inviting ridge
A friendly hand strokes my back, bringing to my attention the scenes below
Humans passing by, lean, fat, tall and also short, time now to preen

133

fur

With clean whiskers, amidst the elements of the day's infuriating irri-
tations

Purring with newfound happiness for now, due to my explorations
and reputation

To keep, a lady friend serene has been found, humans name a
queen

Nature, visualising the scene, a miracle was performed, a new life
begins

Now reigning supreme king and queen of the garden

Reflecting on the human view, I will always be that ginger cat from
next door

Whom they love or hate, starvation beginning to bite, a home is in
order to the family

That love and greet me so it is purrs of contentment, cuddles with a
welcome dish of food

What a sight, curling upon the carpet 'til nature's yearnings unite me
once again

With morning's restored shafts of light

Eileen Mills, Andover, Hampshire

LOVE IN A RAINDROP

Together we have touched the raindrops
of the sky from which they part.
And in doing so, we have also
captured life's love, its beauty and art.

The moon shines so beautiful
and bright over the horizon of the Northern Sea.
And, as I lay here watching,
my heart and thoughts are truly with thee.

I look up to the softness and delicateness
of the clouds in that sky.
But all I see is the caring tenderness
that shows so much in your eye.

I smell, I also breathe the cool
fresh dew of the morning spring.
Within me I feel the pleasure and happiness
in my heart that only you can bring.

I listen to the sweet song
of the morning birds.
But within me I only hear the sound
of your comforting words.

I may feel the cool winter's snow beneath my feet.
But within me I can only feel the warmth of your heart when we
meet.
When I'm with you my heart feels so free.
My darling, my darling I truly love thee.

In our separation who knows where
those raindrops may wander.
Inside of me I feel that in absence
our hearts will only grow fonder.

We will always touch
those raindrops of the sky from which they part.
And, for this reason, we will never
lose this love, the beauty and its art.

Annette Taylor, Irthlingborough, Northamptonshire

SELF DESTRUCTION

The recent wealth of destruction caused by mother nature
Unleashing her wrath
To avenge against man's pure greed of earth
By destroying everything in her path
Huge fires raging for miles alighting the smoke filled skies
Covering the tall chimneys, as if to disguise
To raging spewing volcanoes with thunderous earthquakes
Leaving a deep devastation of destruction in its after wake

Tsunamis flooding whole coastlines and for miles inland
Destroying trees and animals, habitats all gone
Sweeping ahead with such velocity totally out of control
Cars and houses left, not where they should belong
Car carcases mounting pavements
Houses floating down the street
Scenes like an image from a movie
People wandering helplessly looking for loved ones to greet

Ripping the heart out a village, town and city
As the ruins of its soul lay mounted on the ground
Tear strewn faces cling to hope
Looking longingly and lovingly all around
The emptiness inside is too hard to comprehend
How could this happen to us our contented life we did depend
What future is there trying to understand
Placed on the heart there is a single hand

This is mother natures response
To our pollution in the air
For man's mining for coal
Deep into the crust of earth's fragile layer
Drilling deep down to pilfer oil
Fuel for our man-made needs
Landscapes displaying shafts high on the skyline
Spoiling great landscapes for machinery to feed

Our delicate planet of this we should share
To enjoy the creation as species revolve
They have the ability to acclimatise to their new environment
Yet man continues to destroy this before they have a chance to
evolve
By chopping down our landscape
Our forests and our woods
Removing habitats for our flora and fauna
Uprooting new growth, bulbs and buds

How far can we continue to feel it is we who have the power
To pilfer from our land and sea

To sustain our over-population
To house us and to feed
So let us use the wind, water and the sun
Utilise what mother nature is offering us for free
Lets stop exploiting this earth
Stop these futile wars and unite in harmony

Elizabeth Stockhill, Doncaster, South Yorkshire

ECLIPSE '99

Eclipsing the sun in August,
The year '99 proclaims.
To partially darken the Earth it must,
This fleeting mystic show entertains.

Clusters of people on coastline,
Hilltops and gardens galore.
Across Britain - west, south, east they line,
Awaiting the darkness in awe.

Lifetime experience, not to be missed.
For once seen, the mind is retaining,
A heavenly wonder such as this,
To recall through our years remaining.

It was a chance of last century's fate.
That our generation is shown,
A wondrous sight on this date.
To see stars, near noon, when daylight has flown.

Positioned were we in front of TV,
For cloud had obscured our view.
Through a wonder of science, we eagerly see,
The eclipse from our living rooms too.

Sun, Moon and Earth align.
Earth's creatures and plants think it's night!
This darkness reveals in our time,

The awesome sight of galaxy night.

Eclipse of the sun that morn,
On the eleventh, month eight, ninety nine.
The time - some hours past dawn.
After two minutes of night; welcome sunshine.

Terence Crowley, Coggeshall, Essex

GRADUATION DAY

To fill one's heart with glee,
Is to see your child be presented
With their degree
And them dressed in their gown
It makes you so glad to be around.

One of the biggest struggles, heartaches
And nightmares of all,
Is trying to get them into the right local school
Because even if you live in the same village or town
Your authorities can give the places
To those who don't live close around.

You tend to forget all the sleepless nights
And the homework fights.
The doors getting slammed
When they're in a jam,
The deadlines to meet
When they're asleep on their feet.

Then we're pacing up and down,
Waiting for the results to come around
And them with their mood swings,
One minute they're like a rocket blasting off in the air,
Next they're in the depths of despair.

Before you know it, they're off to college,
Or sixth form to get three A levels, or more.

Then we run round the country
Looking at universities galore
And they're still not quite sure.

Now the fun really begins
Of course you've got to kit them out
With pots, pans, sheets and things
And anything that's not screwed to the floor,
Or they can't lift and carry it out of the door.

That's their pay-back day,
I don't suppose I would have it any other way.
I am still not sure whether it's their big day, or ours
As you peel back the hours.

David A. Smith, Weybridge, Surrey

THE WINTER CHILD

In mankind's memory
There has always been a babe, born at midwinter,
From ages unnumbered and unknown.
When mankind lived in caves and feared the world
A child was born in the darkest days
To be a hunter for the tribe,
A boy-child, bringing hope.

There has always been a babe, born in midwinter,
Through pre-history and after,
When mankind worshipped many gods,
A goddess bore a babe signifying hope,
A boy-child, in the dark;
To be a king in summer.

There has always been a babe born in midwinter;
His mother had many names,
Astarte and Aphrodite, Isis and others,
Or simply, *The Goddess*, and her son
Born in the days of darkness,

A boy-child, child of hope.

Jesus was born in Bethlehem,
Strange things remembered of His birth ...
His mother, pregnant when unwed,
Travelling for her travail
In the dark stable; birth ... of a boy-child
And angels singing in the midnight sky.

So when the early Church, 2000 years ago
Had to devise festivals and feasts
To change a hundred faiths to one ...
God's people worshipping His only Son
Who came to earth to die ...
That son had first to be born.
And so they set His birthday in midwinter,
Child of the darkest days;
For mankind already worshipped such a babe,
Sign of hope to the world.

Is it only a myth, then?
Only a memory of other times?
No. Look behind the legends
And the earlier faiths, to the truth,
God does not break his own laws.
There has always been a babe, born in midwinter,
And each new babe has always been a sign of hope.
Only this last, beyond His death, knew resurrection
And is the Saviour of the world.
Jesus - born in midwinter, which we now call Christmas.

Avril Lansdell, Westbury-on-Severn, Gloucestershire

EVENING

I stand, leaning with my elbows on the little rustic bridge.
Alone with my thoughts, while the shadows lengthen all around me.
Looking into the dark moonlit water, broken only by the gleaming
white spray as it rushes over the rocks,

I imagine, somewhere on the sandy bottom,
Fish lie hiding in the shadow of the weeds.
The weeping willow's leafy arms hang down the grassy bank
As if caressing the water, while the reeds bend their heads
As if listening to the whispers of the breeze.
There is a sudden plop as a water rat scurries from his hole,
And pounces on some unsuspecting prey.
The eerie twit-twoo of the owl,
Echoes through the trees, and its two great round eyes
Peer ceaselessly around.
A bat swoops down from the sky with a pathetic little squeak.
I love this time of day, when the air is drowsy and peaceful.
Suddenly, a cold breeze blows, making the over-hanging leaves rustle against each other, I shiver.
The dusk is drawing to a close, and the cold dark night has begun.

Margaret Jorgensson, Stockport, Manchester

MY MOTHER'S THINGS

With heavy heart I went thro' your things Mam.
The finality I just couldn't face.
Not much to show for a lifetime darling,
But richer by far than the gold of kings
The treasures I found as I went thro' your things.

Faded photographs and old birthday cards
Some scarves, some gloves, a brooch that you loved
There were crochet hooks and knitting needles
Some odd balls of wool, a packet of seeds,
An old ration book you couldn't discard.

I remember the wool and what you made,
A ball of purple from a suit for me,
Sent thro' the post with a letter that said,
Wear it my love, I made every stitch,
I never wore it, the guilt I feel still.

Your best effort yet was in putrid green

A massive bedspread you couldn't control,
Only the top of your head to be seen
As you disappeared 'neath the big fat folds
This was a present to your youngest son.

And every cold winter out came the spread
Keeping him cosy and snug in his bed,
We who had mocked left out in the cold
With our fancy duvets, no spread to hold.
He was such a delicate child, you said.

I found your old prayer book shabby with use,
A cream lace mantilla you brought home from Lourdes,
Your rosary beads lonely for your touch
Just as we mam, who still love you so much,
Fond memories too precious to lose.

I pack your belongings away with care,
With your dear family these gems I'll share
The legacy you left - priceless as pearls.
Two quiet, strong people, Paddy and Bride
Now rest together on the green mountainside.

My beloved parents.

Catherine Moran, London, Greater London

LANCELOT AND GUINEVER

Young Arthur was born at Tintagel Court
Now round table leader at Camelot fort
So shaped to avoid position strife
All knights equal in life
To King Arthur the Queen's affair told
By knights of old
Who spied Queen Guinever and Sir Lancelot
Making love at Camelot
King Arthur shouted, *Death to him
Who takes my Queen at his whim*

Sir Mordred came with knights to kill
King Arthur wept at blood-spill
All slain by Sir Lancelot's sword
Sir Mordred escaped to more homely board
King Arthur and Sir Gawayne plans laid
War against Sir Lancelot made
They laid siege to castle length
Once show of Sir Lancelot's strength
Entreat to send Queen back to the King
Then Sir Lancelot a lover's lament did sing
Over the seas he sailed away
With knights to whom he held sway
King Arthur and Sir Gawayne prepared a boat
To catch their enemies afloat
Making land Sir Lancelot was anger filled
So did battle and Sir Gawayne was killed
With King Arthur in mortally wounded pain
On battlefield Sir Mordred lay slain
King Arthur ordered that his sword, Excaliber by name
To be thrown into waters whence it came
He swore Excaliber would be no other's gain
There he lay free from pain
Sir Belvedere found him next morn dead
In pursuit of the Queen Sir Lancelot had fled
Alas he found her dead, to love no more
In grief he carried body to Glastonbury Tor
Thoughts returned of happy times at Camelot
The days of Queen Guinever and Sir Lancelot
And knights of the round table
In their quest for Holy Grail whenever able
The cup used by Jesus for last time
Joseph collected blood in cup at crucifixion crime
Legend has it written
That he brought it to Britain
Sir Lancelot became sick, body shaken
To his beloved castle he was taken
Sir Ecktor found his brother Sir Lancelot dead
Where oft the Queen he did bed
Sir Lancelot and knights never found the grail

But enjoyed adventures along the trail

David K Maxwell, Bristol, Avon

MOTHER

A mother who is alive is a saint and not a sinner,
Whether she has experience or whether she's a beginner,
There is one thing you can count on and that's she'll always be
there,
To pick you up and nurse you and give you tender loving care.

But when she's gone you miss her and you appreciate her more,
When you get back home she won't be waiting at the door,
She's gone up to Heaven now with all the others,
By saying this to you, I mean other peoples' mothers.

Your mother won't be there anymore to say what she has to say,
So you can do what you want now, you can play away,
But know one thing she's watching you from Heaven's pearly gate,
There she'll stand still lovingly without a feeling of hate.

Mothers are forgiving they always are,
If you need to get somewhere, she'd take you in the car,
Learn to appreciate her, learn to stay in touch,
Remember she's your mother, she never asks for much.

Georgia Machin, Kingham, Oxfordshire

FARNEY CLOSE TO 4 WEST

In October of 1976
I went to Farney Close
Down near Haywards Heath, Sussex
Because parents were not close
The bully boys told me that
The yellow van was coming
To put me in a home
For 'flids', 'spastics' and 'hummings'

It was no yellow van
But a green bus instead
Bearing the name Wigston Coaches
To work in WDC dread
The bully boys at Farney Close
Seemingly had won the fight
Paid only pocket-money wages
Worked from 1983 to 2011
Now back in work circulation
So have those bully boys really won?

Hugh Griffiths, Market Harborough, Leicestershire

BLUE DOORS ARE FASTER

I broke my sledge some time last year, the beech tree there it
stopped my run.
Lengthwise snapped poorly made I fear, that terminated last year's
fun.
But the runners OK did appear, homeward took when I was done.

I did not mend it straight away, I know I should but distractions
come;
More important things, I say, *Summertime - a sledge is dumb.*
Leave its repair another day. The snow has fallen and I'm glum.

Simon's Scrap Yard I then go, a sledging top is what I need.
Something strong I want, you know, the geezer said look with all
speed.
An old blue door I soon had in tow, and a fair price we agreed.

I lugged it home, what a weight. The door was long, the runners
short.
Cutting it I knew I'd hate. I fitted them on what I'd bought.
Overhangs the same create. Holes for steering rope I thought.

Of course, by now the snow had gone. Served me right my Mum
crowed.
Last year was when repairs were done. But January it soon snowed,

To Garrard's Hill I went for fun, and to the hill it soon was towed.

It ran so true and fast and straight, the sweetest sledge I declare.
So many runs, I couldn't wait, Peter said it really wasn't fair.
It made his speedster looking late. But I said I didn't care.

My mates all wanted to have a go I charged them 20p a run.
I cleared what I'd paid you know and made a tidy little sum.
Jimmy looked at it just so, *What if the handle is undone?*

Just let it be. I growled at him - removing it would be a waste.
But does it work? How like Jim and he opened it in haste.
He slipped and fell inside the rim, over him shut door post-haste.

I moved the sledge no Jimmy there, to our surprise he'd vanished quite.
To say that it gave us a scare Jimmy had gone and we were fright.
That blue door wasn't very fair - it went back to scrap that night.

                              Peter Young, Watford, Greater London

LOVE'S TIGHT ROPE

Deep and meaningful, I tried to be there
You had my heart but ripped it apart
The years of breathing and interlocking seeking
Relay races and steeple chases

The bar raised high; well that's what I thought.
You never once asked and you didn't offer any reason.

Afraid to look me in the eye then tell a string of lies
You played the silent, hiding game; behind the peeping glass
The knife edge stabs me quick and sharp, perforating my heart
As I turned, on my heels, I look up to see; my world caving in.

I stepped back holding the jigsaw of my chest
Squeezing tightly to all pieces with the hope they'll all fit.
Why me, why us and for what reason?

I could not ask or was it the season?

I gave it my all, too much to bear
Then had it thrown back and crushed this way
Too naive to see through the gaps of pain
Never thought I would be at the tail end

The beautiful glade the wind took my sail
The highs and lows had me amazed
Sailing far and wide and to the furthest corners
Hammered and stapled; very puzzled

The bees around the honey pot will bite
Working their hearts off, seeing no light
Do you think it right that twist of the knife?
Do you think it right another human turned inside out?

The heat off my organ moves fearsomely
Too immature to see the cliff edge peek
The trust I installed you've shattered this day
Blurry eyed, mixed up mind. I don't know how I'm to survive

We've both grown apart and matured with others
Stretching our wings far and wide, taking in many lessons
After the bud was severed; never thought it would ever blossom
You still haven't made good and asked ... or given a complete reason.

Suzette Lindsay, Bermondsey, Greater London

£1,000 to the winner

All top poets never miss sending an annual entry for the National Poetry Anthology. Even if you have won through previously, and had your poetry published in it, this free competition is always open to you. And as it's the only big free poetry competition of its kind, it's the first one you should put on your list to submit your work to. It's the biggest free annual poetry competition in the UK. Around 250 winners are selected every year, each one representing a different UK town. All winners are published in the National Poetry Anthology and all receive a free copy of the book. Many of these poets have never been published before. Send up to THREE poems (on any subject) up to 25 lines and 160 words each (a blank line counts as one line), by the annual closing date of **June 30th** to - United Press Ltd Admail 3735, London EC1B 1JB Tel 0844 800 9177 *www.unitedpress.co.uk* One overall winner also receives a cheque for £1,000 and the National Poetry Champion Trophy.

Another £1,000 to be won

A poem about someone or something from your home town can win you a top prize in this annual competition. Anyone can submit up to three poems for the competition. The top poem will win £1,000 cash. There is no age limit and no entry fee.

"The poem can be about something or someone from the poet's home area," explained United Press Publications Director, Peter Quinn. "It can be descriptive, historic, romantic, political, or personal - anything you like, as long as there is some local connection.This competition is open to anyone and is completely free to enter - so what have you got to lose?"

Send up to THREE poems, up to 25 lines and 160 words each (a blank line counts as one line), by the annual closing date of December 31st to the above address.

Welcome to the Short Story Society

Even if you have never had any prose published before, you should submit something to the Short Story Society.

It's the perfect platform for your writing talents and gives you a fantastic opportunity to get your work published. Our aim is to help writers to create short stories and get them published and appreciated.
There's no membership fee to join the Society.
To be a member you must submit a short story. You must then have that story accepted by us. If we do accept it, we will publish it in a compilation of short stories by several authors and give you five copies of the book.
We will also put your story on our website at shortstorysociety.co.uk for visitors to read and enjoy - in the months leading up to the publication of the finished book. We will also give you 40 per cent discount if you want to produce your own book. Having a short story published is a wonderful and inspirational learning process for all authors - especially those who have never had their prose published before.

Your next step is to submit a short story. It could be handwritten or it could be typewritten. It could be on email or any kind of disc. You should send it to:
The Short Story Society
United Press Ltd
Admail 3735 London EC1B 1JB
www.shortstorysociety.co.uk
email - info@shortstorysociety.co.uk
phone - 0844 800 9177
fax - 0844 800 9178
Your story can be on any subject.
It can be aimed at children, it can be a ghost story, it can be a love story, a horror story, a true life story.

NEW BOOK IS A BOOST FOR BARNARDO'S

Don't you wish you'd written down some of the funny things you've heard kids say?

Well someone has - and they've put them all in a book to help raise cash for Barnardo's.

"Things Kids Say" is out now (£5.99) and half of the cover price goes straight to the well-known children's charity. This hilariously funny book was launched by actress and TV celebrity Lynda Bellingham at a Barnardo's centre, and it includes 130 pages of comical real things that have been said by real kids - along with illustrations.

"The book proves that kids are by far the best comedians. All the submissions have been provided by people from all over the UK and all the 13 artists gave their services free," said Peter Quinn, managing director of United Press, which has published the book.

"To cut out the middle-man and make sure that as much of the revenue as possible goes to Barnardo's, we aren't selling the book in shops. You must order it direct."

For your copy, send £5.99 (plus £1.99 postage & packing) made out to 'United Press' to United Press, Admail 3735, London, EC1B 1JB. £3 from every copy sold goes direct to Barnardo's. Postage is free if you order two or more copies.

To order by credit/debit card phone 0844 800 9177.